REAL WOMEN WRITE:

Living on COVID Time

FOREWORD BY
Brooke Warner

EDITED BY
Susan F. Schoch

**SHARING STORIES, SHARING LIVES
IN PROSE AND POETRY FROM
STORY CIRCLE NETWORK**

Story Circle
NETWORK
by, for, and about women.

A Publication of Story Circle Network

Real Women Write: Living on COVID Time
Sharing Stories, Sharing Lives
in Prose and Poetry from Story Circle Network
Volume 19, 2020

ISBN: 978-0-9795329-6-2

Story Circle Network
723 W University Ave #300-234
Georgetown TX 78626

https://www.storycircle.org

Real Women Write is an annual anthology of writings by Story Circle Network members, including nonfiction, fiction, and poetry. It appears in December in both print and digital forms, showcasing the talent and creativity of SCN writing women.

Story Circle Network values every woman's story, and in *Real Women Write* we publish writing about both the individual life in all its uniqueness, and a woman's life as it's understood by all women.

Foreword by Brooke Warner

Edited by Susan F. Schoch

Cover image, interior design, and technical support by Sherry Wachter

"Even in hard times, our stories

help cement our values and strengthen our connections.

Sharing them shows us the way forward."

— Michelle Obama

Contents

NATURE

WRONGS

TIME

A TRANSFORMATION

FOREWORD
Brooke Warner

To remember 2020 will be to look back on a year marked by complexity—so much loss swirled together with surprising gains. For those of us drawn to the page, this time of isolation might have been extremely rich and fecund, or so anxiety-filled that it came with a desire to write that proved fruitless. In normal times, we write from a vantage point of looking back. Baked into the process of writing is an implication that we've landed on the other side of something—experience, understanding. But in this era of COVID, many people are writing about this thing that we're collectively smack-dab in the middle of, lived experience unfolding right in front of us.

If you've ever taken a writing class you've undoubtedly been told to put distance between your past and your processing of what happened. And yet as someone who teaches memoir, I've seen some of the most powerful and raw writing come from writers who are capturing a present moment—writing through hard times, through crisis, through feeling like their world has been upended. This is something COVID is giving us all an opportunity to do.

I've always loved personal stories—essays, memoirs, poetry, and other forms of nonfiction—because writers of these forms must wrestle with what sense they make of experiences. To write about what you've lived through is to process anew, to see something again, this time with fresh perspective. This happens with fiction, too, of course; after all, is there a novelist out there who doesn't draw from their own understanding of a life lived? But what happens when you pull from the *now*, the tender and vulnerable immediacy of a lived moment in time? Perhaps you won't have distance, but you are recording history—a shared history that we will all draw upon and be shaped by for decades to come.

When I teach memoir, I remind my students about the importance of touching their readers' hearts by being attuned to universal emotions—love, grief, fear, rage—and human rites of passage, things like childbirth or losing a loved one. These are things that cut across geography and cultures, experiences that countless humans go through by the simple fact of living a life. COVID is unique in that it's not cyclical. This is not anything our parents lived through before us. There are no guidebooks for how to survive a global pandemic with grace. We're figuring it out as we go. For the introspective among us, and readers and writers almost always are, this has been a moment to take stock. How has the existence of COVID in our lives been triggering? In what ways has it been a relief? Has it brought up feelings of guilt and shame if you've been okay, even better than okay, while others suffer? Has it caused you direct suffering, either because you or someone you love got sick, or even died?

We come to the page for release. To read is to escape, or to seek a different perspective, or to feel something outside of what we're faced with in our day-to-day. To write is to sort things out, to find some sort of organizing principle for all the things we carry, to get things out of our heads. During COVID, everything pertaining to the written word seems to have taken on increased importance. Facing the prospect of death, one begins to assess one's priorities. In the US, this pandemic has also seen a nation grappling with its history of racism and police violence, which is upsetting and agitating, and pushing people to stand up for what they value. We are asking ourselves (hopefully), *What kind of country is this, really? And what kind of country do we want ours to be for generations to come?* Moments of reckoning create zeitgeists, and we're in one, where more people than ever are reading writers of color, and where there's more much-needed and overdue consciousness about white privilege, writing "the other," cultural appropriation, and more.

In the early months of March and April, during the lockdowns in various cities across the globe, there was a sense of living in no-time. There were countless references to Groundhog Day, and a parade of memes that acknowledged the shared reality that this version of the apocalypse was seeing us all isolated at home in our pajamas rather than crossing vast terrain in combat gear as envisioned in movies like *Mad Max* or *Cloud Atlas*. But as the months wore on, new considerations emerged. We saw masked protesters in the streets for days and nights on end, demonstrating to show that sometimes we must make calculated risks and stand up for what matters. Living through this pandemic is creating clarity as it unmasks any false notions we might have held about social and racial equality in these professed United States of America. Living in COVID time has heightened the tensions between those who are invested in the status quo because it serves them and those who desperately seek change because they need to believe in a better future.

The question we might all ask ourselves as we head into our wobbly and uncertain future is, *How will we continue to prioritize what matters?* For those of us who feel drawn to the page, this of course includes our writing. In Zoom rooms this year, I've heard many people give voice to their guilt—for being okay, for having money, for being privileged. A spiritual teacher I admire said in one of these sessions that guilt doesn't help anyone. In a similar vein, we don't all need to suffer in order for this moment to matter. We can't and we don't all suffer equally, or simultaneously. And our energies will be better spent on things that are generative and supportive and that pull us in the direction of what we want to see as we enter a new decade. To me, writing is that generative act, and through reading and convening and connecting we can and will foster the supportive communities we'll all need to get us through this global crisis.

COVID-19 has been called a once-in-a-century epidemic, something no living person has lived through that they can remember, a global pandemic that presents the same existential threats to all of us, whether we reside in the Pacific Northwest, the Deep South, Scandinavia, Sri Lanka, or North Korea. As such, it's humanizing, and humbling. Because it's ongoing and affecting everyone, it's also of this moment in a way few other outside forces can be. We are living on COVID time, and we are living in COVID time.

In this collection of writings, a diverse group of women considers what living in this way means. Their stories showcase a range of reactions to living on COVID time, which include grappling with illness and fear and death, with heartbreak and isolation, with the coexistence of ugliness and beauty. In these pages, you may see yourself. You will surely be moved by the many perspectives and considerations and experiences in this collection. You'll hit highs and lows, which is the very reason we read in the first place—to be transported into others' lives, and in so doing, drink in the rich mixture that is life on planet Earth.

We're living in divided times, in troubling times, in tumultuous times. And yet, if we let them, these trials can help us to see all the ways in which we're more similar than we are different. We are living through a much-needed reckoning—one that is deeply painful, yes, but which may also heal old wounds if we navigate through it with compassion, and if we listen. Reading is one way we listen, and writing is one way we start a conversation with vulnerability. We have an opportunity to live more courageously, and to make what time we have left our most true, our most honest, and our most productive. Let the words you read in this collection inspire you—to write and to be more prolific, to never abandon your heartfelt impulse to create on your own terms, and also to listen, to be an ally, and to enter into others' experiences with an open heart.

Real Women Write: Living on COVID Time is the nineteenth edition of Story Circle Network's annual member anthology, but it's the first edition based on women's writings during a global pandemic. In the spring of 2020, when this subject became almost inevitable, SCN couldn't know what the situation would be by the time of publication. Yet the mission is always clear, to support and encourage women to write about their experience, and this particular experience is both shared and unprecedented. We know that writing is an important tool for health, and a vital way to recognize the truth and significance of women's lives. And we know this herstory will be important for generations to come.

Included here are 80 pieces of prose and poetry by 52 SCN authors responding to the theme "Living on COVID Time."

Brooke Warner says in her Foreword, "To remember 2020 will be to look back on a year marked by complexity—so much loss swirled together with surprising gains."

That swirl is evident in the responses of these authors. The selections represent a cross-section of women's lives as COVID-19 moved from rumor to life-altering reality. They reflect the changing tenor and issues as the year progressed, but they are not presented in that order. Instead, they seem to naturally cluster around shared experiences and feelings, such as Masks, Distance, Fears, Losses, Comforts, Wrongs, and more. Each of these creative expressions is individual, yet each reveals our common humanity, too.

As Michelle Obama says, sharing our stories "shows us the way forward." This has been a year that demands attention to moving forward *together,* and this volume of *Real Women Write* is shaped, in response, by a renewed commitment to inclusion and diversity.

While the anthology includes a generous sampling of entries received, selection is limited. We work hard to choose the best writing—relevant, engaging, worth your time—and also publish writers of varied experience and opportunity. Edited with a light hand, each piece retains the writer's voice. The resulting collection is a remarkable chorus, one that may move you, surprise you, validate or challenge you. We think you'll hear the harmony in it.

We also did not standardize usage for the name of the novel coronavirus, though the official term is COVID-19. Many of us feel that all-caps looks like shouting, and prefer Covid-19. Which quickly becomes Covid. And even covid. The pandemic. Or simply the virus.

Likewise with other new acronyms and words that have become part of our language, such as PPE for Personal Protective Equipment, BLM for Black Lives Matter, or Zooming for any kind of online video gathering. These terms are not yet standardized, and we did not force a rule for them. Eventually history will provide a consensus, but it feels a part of the general uncertainty and confusion for such irregularities to appear unresolved in the language as the year comes to a close. And the variations seem as natural as local dialect to the writers.

It's rewarding and inspiring to work with the fine writers and good women of Story Circle Network, and I'm personally grateful to edit this remarkable anthology. Such a collection does not come together without a strong team. Story Circle Network's founder, Susan Wittig Albert, is a clear-eyed advisor. Jeanne Guy, SCN president, brings insight and leadership to the process, and much-needed laughter. Story Circle's board of directors continues to strongly support this publishing opportunity for SCN members. Sherry Wachter, longtime member and gifted artist, is our designer and digital transformer. All have my deep appreciation and affection. Special gratitude goes to Brooke Warner, publisher at She Writes Press, for her moving and important Foreword. And we're all thankful, as always, to the creative women who submitted their writing, and in doing so have helped to build a valuable collection for readers long into the future.

Real Women Write is especially important for creating connection despite physical distance and isolation during this pandemic. May you find comfort, encouragement, and inspiration in the words of these writing women, as we all move forward together into the mystery of a fresh new year.

SUSAN SCHOCH, EDITOR
Real Women Write: Living on COVID Time

A Beginning

A COVID FAIRYTALE
Elena Schwolsky

Once upon a time…

Wait, no, this story can't start like that.
Once upon a time is for fairytales
Happy ending stories
Not this one.
How else should it start then? Just give it a try.
OK, here goes nothing.

Once upon a time there was a virus.
A parasitic, microscopic, invisible virus looking for a host.
It emerged from the shadows one day.
Ok, ok, good beginning
But who gets to tell this story—the scientists? The politicians?
Who am I to tell this story? Just a person,
one tiny speck on the planet, insignificant,
just a number on a graph,
look for me in the 64-74 years of age category.
I'm in the Western Hemisphere.
Do you see the U.S.? New York City? Can you see Brooklyn? Zip
    code 11220?
Turn left on 47ᵗʰ St. The house with the Japanese Maple in front.
Up the stoop, behind the green door.
There, there that's me.
I'm here,
surviving, waiting, luckier than most.

My body moves from couch to bed to fridge to couch
What day is it? Thursday? Oh good.
On Thursdays I go for a walk down deserted streets,
pulling my body away when I pass a stranger.
Everyone is masked, hiding smiles or frowns,
only their eyes to express what they feel.
What did you do today, my friend asks?

Or, how are you?
No comment, I want to say,
but that would be unkind,
and above all else I want to be kind.

Once upon a time we lost track of the days.
Some of us worried about where our next meal would come from,
while others worried only about when they could get an appointment
    to have groceries delivered.
Some of us worried about paying the rent,
while others got out the vacuum cleaner because the cleaning lady
    couldn't come.

Where was I in all this?
A speck behind a green door,
living my story.
There will be time enough to tell it when the virus returns to the
    shadows.
I hope.

Distance

IMAGINE
Linda Hoye

It's a sunny afternoon near the end of May. A light breeze blows and baskets of multi-colored petunias on a cart at the front of the grocery store wave at shoppers. We queue across the front of the store, standing the requisite six feet apart from one another thanks to yellow tape lines on the sidewalk, waiting our turn to enter the hallowed space and wearing the same stunned look on our faces.

We're on the hunt for yeast that is rarely in stock, meat (two items only per customer), and perishables like milk and yogurt and cheese. Toilet paper and hand sanitizer? Forget it. There's none to be found. The supply of flour is unusually low so we will grab a bag whether we need it or not. So, too, the ice cream. We're all in need of comfort, and food gives us a measure of it.

We move forward at regular, spaced intervals. The wait won't be long. It's an opportunity to enjoy a few minutes outside on a warm spring afternoon. It would be another matter altogether if we were standing in line on a cold, dark, Canadian winter day in temperatures of -24 Celsius (that's -11 Fahrenheit). Whichever scale you choose, it's not weather one wants to be outside in for long, but as it is now, in late spring, the wait is pleasant. Or at least I can talk myself into believing that's the case.

The arrows and one-way aisles still confuse me and I cheat the system occasionally. I haven't been able to understand the flow and, frankly, decided it's not worth the tax on my mental health to continue to try. I do the best I can. There's still the dance with other shoppers to avoid stepping into someone's space, the irritation at those who linger too long causing a bottleneck to form behind them, and the pressure to grab-and-go so as not to hold up another shopper. There's the discomfit of this new world where some people wear face masks and others don't, where plexiglass partitions separate customers from staff, and carefully spaced decals on the floor remind shoppers of the safe distance to stay back from the person in front.

Some who are quarantined, self-isolating, or just not comfortable going out in public have their groceries delivered; others take advantage of curbside pickup. I've maintained an in-person shopping practice, freeing up the delivery spaces for those who need it and also because it tricks me into experiencing a semblance of normalcy in the middle of that which is anything but.

Two long-haired young women are in line in front of me. They're obviously together. We're supposed to shop alone—one person per family unit—to give everyone an opportunity in stores where capacity is limited, so this grates on me a bit, but I let it go. There are so many things that grate these days, and this is the least of my concerns. One woman reaches into her pocket and pulls out her phone. She looks out over the parking lot as she speaks into it.

"Oh, yes. I see you," she says.

Someone must have dropped them off and gone to find a place to park. It's what we do now. We're either the person waiting in the car or the person braving the store. In our household we decided two months ago, when this whole pandemic thing upset life as we knew it, that I'd do the shopping because my husband is in a higher risk category. I'm thankful I stockpile groceries as a regular practice and I have a well-stocked larder thanks to summer canning and freezing activities. I keep a long list and infrequently, only when necessary, muster the courage to stand in line and brave entering the grocery store. It's one of the few times I leave the house.

Sometimes we take a drive in the afternoon for a change of scenery, other times I putter unenthusiastically in my community garden plot, but most of the time I stay home doing jigsaw puzzles, reading, writing, or playing with watercolor paint (an activity I took up as my pandemic hobby) trying not to let the news overwhelm me.

Back in late March, a trip to the grocery store meant carving out time to decompress in the car afterward. It meant allowing pent up emotion to leak from my eyes before I put my key in the ignition to drive home past cordoned off playgrounds and shops with "closed" signs in windows. Now I'm used to it. Or at least it's less likely to send me to a dark place.

I'd like to think the shared experience of a worldwide pandemic would draw us together as human beings, but I see ample evidence to the contrary. There are paper hearts in windows and chalk drawings with encouraging messages on sidewalks and armies of people in their homes sewing fabric facemasks for frontline workers, but there's also fear, distrust, and finger-pointing. People stand on balconies making noise to acknowledge the effort of healthcare professionals and others turn into self-appointed judges, never missing an opportunity to denigrate someone who expresses a viewpoint contrary to their own.

I think we can talk ourselves into believing and getting used to a lot of things. Forty years ago, I got used to something I should have never accepted. Life with an alcoholic, abusive spouse wasn't easy. I never lost my longing for something different, but it got to the point where dysfunction felt normal to me. Like I said, we can get used to anything. It took a few years living on my own, therapy, and a second marriage to a man polar opposite to my first husband for me to recognize the level of dysfunction I saw as normal. I couldn't have imagined what my life would become, and now, I can't imagine ever living that way again.

These days we're all forced to reckon with changes in our daily life we could never have imagined. Maybe the fact that we're experiencing it together makes it easier. We're told the restrictions are necessary— not forever, just for now—but it doesn't stop our longing for life as it was. I wonder how long it will be until we are in, what they're calling, the "new normal." I wonder if we'll forget what it's like in these dark days. I wonder if those who come after us will say they can't imagine living in a time when we quarantined, self-isolated, socially distanced; when all but businesses deemed "essential" closed their doors; when schools were closed and parents who still had jobs worked from home; when the toll on our mental health was great; when we monitored our physical health for symptoms of the virus; when "stay safe" replaced "have a nice day" as the standard greeting; and when we all tried to figure out which truth was the real truth. I think they will.

I can't imagine it, and I'm living through it.

BEFORE OUR COVID SUMMER
Christine Ristaino

We're sitting at the table outside, and I can tell Dad's going to spill out this pearl. He doesn't say much, but every time I visit, he comes up with one of these bits of wisdom, carefully rationed to make it worth the wait.

A few years before, during a particularly difficult time, he had reassured me, "The only thing that's constant is change." But now, it's a happier time. We're all together and we spend the week telling stories. They are the same ones as last year and the year before, only more embellished. The fish that was caught, larger than I remember. Dad locking himself in the car, found by his neighbor who just happened to be passing by. Mom walking innocently through the house with a new spiral cookie saying, "Nut Twist anyone?" Inevitably, my four brothers do something altogether predictable in its unpredictability. This visit they begin to speak with different made-up accents, giving bogus medical advice.

Sometimes I go to bed earlier than they do and through the window I hear them out there, erupting into laughter, storytelling, and occasional beer-inflicted cursing, their conversations melodic, easing me to sleep like a bedtime story.

Dad and I are outside sitting at the table. There's a breeze and the sun is peeking through the trees in the backyard. Everyone else is sleeping. We're locked in comfortable silence, reading on the porch. Finally, he turns to me. "It's not the bad times that hurt when you think about them years later," he says. "It's the good times, the best times. They are so rare, and when you think about them, they sting."

This COVID summer is the first in years that we haven't gathered together as a family. All I can think of is that moment, that pearl of a conversation, a simple gem that stings when I think about it.

MY NEW REALITY
Charlotte Wlodkowski

The first time I heard your name was in late March of this year. We were told you came for a visit and would leave shortly. You fooled me and the whole world. You put your footprint in every town, in every state, and in every country. It did not occur to me how drastically my world would change because of you.

At the time, we were given to think you left, but that was just a tease. I think you were hiding so more of us would be lax. Then, you attacked us viciously to gain more control.

In trying to protect its people, our leadership has imposed protocols. I believe we Americans follow the rules without much defiance. However, you won't give up and go away. As a result of your lingering, it's disturbing and frightening to witness business owners closing their doors and losing their livelihood. Every person has their own frustrations. The following are my restraints.

Going in and out of stores requires wearing a mask. Never having worn a mask of any kind, it is difficult to continue this procedure. It always forces me to remember to have a mask with me and to not touch my face. When acknowledging a person, I can't see their expression. Are they smiling? It dehumanizes us.

Taking joy out of life is concerning. I have second thoughts of ever going to a coffee shop with a friend, which at one time I thoroughly enjoyed.

Every other month, I would schedule a lunch date with those I worked with in the past. We looked forward to keeping in touch. We would share stories and recent pictures. It's not the same over the phone or on the computer.

I was harshly told my family must remain at a distance. There could be no more gatherings, no more singing Happy Birthday and clapping as a young one tries to blow out every candle. There is no more laughing at silly jokes or tasting the newest recipe. Family game nights have been curtailed. It is painful not to be able to show caring to a relative with a big hug. I am falling into a depression.

Being able to attend a fundraiser, go to a movie theater, or visit a museum exhibit is high on my list. Since I retired, I look forward to those entertainment activities. They have been taken away.

Because we are advised to stay indoors, my clothes have been mismatched. My face is bare of any makeup. When I do need to go out, it has become stressful to make myself presentable.

Living in a friendly neighborhood, we used to exchange food. I sometimes cooked too much for one person, so would gladly hand a container of extras to one of my neighbors and they would do the same. It gave us an opportunity to talk and share friendship. I miss that.

Through all this, I've gained weight. Eating at night is the cause. I know not to do it, but I'm anxious.

I am grateful for one thing, that my Mother is no longer here. At ninety-two, she needed a walker, had arthritis in her hands, and tired easily. It was my pleasure to cook, clean, and grocery shop for her. How would I have taken care of my dear Mother, as she lived alone in a high-rise apartment?

My life is now consumed with information on the virus. Every news station and every talk show are delivering confusing statistics. My mind is beginning to shut down, almost in an impassive state.

I remember the days when I could speak my mind without fear of retaliation. I felt respected. People listened. We could discuss things with manners, logic, and reasoning. That is all gone.

I miss my otherwise normal American life. When I think of what I could do in the past and compare it with the right now, I feel like a prisoner. Some of us are losing faith in the data that is being shared. Some of us are recalling past pandemics and wondering why this one is so different. Others are spewing hate talk about the Chinese, saying that country created COVID-19 in hopes of destroying our economy.

It's problematic to understand what is truly going on. At the beginning, I put my trust in our officials. But lately, it seems we are being told a little of this and a little of that just to keep us under control. That is not a good feeling. I recently heard that if one sees someone or a business not following the rules, they should be reported. It brought back memories of Nazi Germany. Are we headed in this direction? I sincerely hope not.

I feel empty inside.

ISOLATED IN PARADISE
Merimée Moffitt

You singing karaoke in our den, alone
Kids skating in the streets, doing Ollies
like never before
What you said about getting in bed
—no strings
John baring his soul like James Baldwin
Me planting tomatoes, third year,
in the fishpond from my own starter seeds
A bed of zinnias for the bees
Families out of the woodwork biking
walking with strollers, empty parks
Compliance like poppy seeds dotting fear
In our big house we shift apart, either
we sell or someone moves in
Too much space for us, too much garden
So many good meals created, you
doing your share. The deliveries have been
helpful but they too will end
The air is pristine like fifty years ago;
ecstasy. We got lucky finding
crackers and popcorn, online to our steps
No one has touched our door in five weeks
isolation, in paradise
CNN shows scenes from the Russian Ballet, a
canceled spring performance, from their homes
Your man body benefits from work in the garden
I find my three hole punch, at last!
The funny ad for personal lubricant on TV—
We laugh together; you are shocked, having
missed the Sixties doing soldiering, the Seventies
drinking a sea of discomfort, the Eighties making
babies with me
The covid print, Chicago hot dog mustard-color
The kids' show put on by Broadway from Home!
Our granddaughter rocked her stuff to the world
You wake up from a long dream
and when you sing now, I know we're good to go

In Paradise #2
Merimée Moffitt

Relentless crickets embed in fickle wind, wildly clattering
the *joie de vivre* of Outside. Through cluttered rooms, the breezes
flutter curtains, rock pictures on the wall.

Outside, the porch's arched windows open for the season
encourage the nostalgia of June bugs and beetles
the new scarcity of flying creatures

I recall the Cooper's hawk this afternoon, perched
on the handles of the floatie in our big baby pool, the bird
gazing like Narcissus into the rippling clear water, then sudden flight.

My bike came home from the shop tuned up with new tires.
Tomorrow the Air Pressure Lord may consider them acceptable.
At least he wears a mask, as do most of us in this 'hood.

My earthbound days are housebound now, attached
to the new baby coming along soon. On a picnic at the creek,
Randy identifies an Arizona Sister butterfly in the verdant Sandias.

I recall my father in his last days of cancer, expounding on the glory
of a Santa Monica day. His house tucked into a cul de sac with
alleys to the beach dripping bougainvillea and honeysuckle vines.

Our government failed us during AIDS. Citizens so hellbent
on blaming and ignoring, apparently terrified of man
love, afraid of pleasure in their ridiculous white privilege pants.

My brother was swept away, too late for the scientists' magic,
too young to die. He'd open his tall windows and welcome city sounds,
people singing in the street, horns, sirens, cold winter air

caressing his Italian glass, mussing his silver hair, a trade up
from the thatch of California dirty blonde, now bleached silver-white.
He said he wasn't sure if the ailments were of aging or from AIDS, at 48.

And so he slipped away. We don't speak of that pandemic. We get on
    with our
desire to survive the infantile madman at the helm. An all angel alert,
    again
and we cling, stoically, to the bobbing raft of you, of me, of each other.

A NURSE IN THE TIME OF CONTAGION
Elena Schwolsky

A Facebook post reminds me that today, May 6, is the start of National Nurses Week and tonight the sound of clanging, banging, and clapping outside my window will summon me to step out to my stoop. I will open my door and join the salute to our essential workers in this, the Covid-19 global pandemic of 2020. We are paying tribute to them all—the doctors, the grocery clerks, the home health aides, the postal carriers, the cleaners and subway workers—all who are helping us survive this disaster. But each time my wooden spoon hits the flame-burnished copper bottom of my old pot, I think of the nurses. They appear on TV with hollow eyes and the red marks left by their masks etched on their faces, and I know in my bones the weariness they feel, the ache in their hearts, the deeper scars that will fade but never quite disappear when they finally step off the frontlines. Age and health and years away from hospital work compel me to sit this one out, but I too served in the trenches during a far different plague in a different moment in history. Clang, clang, clang— I beat out a rhythm on my pot for the nurses—it's about time! It's about time, it's about fucking time.

When the last ringing notes of my downstairs neighbor's brass bell have faded, I sit for a while longer on the stoop, watching the clouds on the horizon turn pink and then disappear in the gathering dark. My thoughts drift back to my own time as a nurse. In 1988, I joined the staff of the Children's Hospital AIDS Program (CHAP) in Newark, New Jersey, and enlisted in the fight against a disease that was growing rapidly into a worldwide plague. I was not a new nurse, nor was I a young one. I had not been a girl who dreamed of becoming a nurse from childhood. My senior yearbook lists my career aspirations as writer, actress, and interpreter at the United Nations. But after dropping out of college to be a full-time activist in the late '60s, and a series of low paying factory and clerical jobs, I found myself approaching thirty as a single mom with no marketable skills and two kids to support. Nursing school seemed like a reasonable choice. I graduated in 1980, spent some years accumulating experience on the pediatric wards of several hospitals, and then stepped into the vortex of the early years of the AIDS epidemic.

That early plague had its deniers and spreaders of lies just like this one. The virus that caused it was a mystery, new to the world of humans just like this one. And it appeared that certain groups in our human family were more susceptible, though at the beginning no one knew why. That plague came on more slowly, in what at first seemed like random clusters—young gay men in San Francisco and New York City, IV drug users, Haitian immigrants, and a small number of hemophiliacs and blood transfusion recipients—until it gathered speed and rolled over the world. Soon those who were infected would be divided into the *victims*—those who were deemed innocent and without fault—and the *guilty*, condemned for bringing it on themselves by their deviant, sinful, or reckless behavior. Much like now, we had a President who, instead of providing leadership and compassion, refused to even speak the name of the disease until it had ravaged a generation.

Everyone was terrified at first. Could it be spread by sitting across from someone at the dinner table, by hugging someone, by a casual peck on the cheek, a handshake? Unlike Covid-19, the Human Immunodeficiency Virus (HIV) could not be transmitted by any of those activities. In fact, it was very difficult to transmit. But that didn't stop the fear, the stigma and discrimination that marked those early years and persist to this day. And that fear and stigma drifted like a cloud of acrid smoke over the heads of the nurses who chose to care for those who were suffering and dying. We wrapped ourselves in protective gear much like the nurses of today—gowns and masks and gloves that got in the way when we needed to make a bed, hold a hand, or shed a tear. And when someone at a party asked, "*What kind of work do you do?*" we tried not to get upset when the conversation ended abruptly and they walked away. The families we worked with faced much harsher responses when they were found out—kids thrown out of school or daycare, loss of jobs or housing, estrangement from family and community.

There were no 7 PM salutes in the early '90s—just nurses bathing feverish bodies, dressing wounds, bearing witness. Just nurses going to too many funerals. Just nurses unable to talk about anything else, or keeping silent. Just nurses crying in the night, or not crying at all.

The streetlights illumine a lone dog-walker across the street as I rise from the concrete steps and shake out my stiff legs. I will go in and fix dinner, and my life partner and I will sit alone at our long dining table and try to talk about something other than our longing to see our grandkids or our fear that friends will get sick. We haven't gone farther than the stoop in two months.

The street is empty as I close the door behind me, but it will be filled with neighbors at 7 PM tomorrow. From our stoops, from the sidewalk, from top-floor windows, on our block and all over the city, we will be there to show our thanks and appreciation. And I will stand on my top step tomorrow night and every night, clanging away for the nurses on the frontlines of this Covid-19 pandemic—glad that they are being recognized for the courageous, compassionate heroes that they are—and that nurses have been throughout history.

REPRIEVE FOR MOTHER EARTH
Sarah Fine

Escape
there is none
or so they say
flights and cruises cancelled
a reprieve for mother earth
a slowdown of climate change

Escape
from the news
24/7 coronavirus
global pandemic
have all the wars stopped
or are we in a bubble
self isolated from climbing death tolls
a culling of the old, the vulnerable

Escape
rooms were
all the rage
at least
we were entertained
while being locked inside
now the door is open
but the danger is outside
how much more prudent
to lay low
stay put
hunker down
the opposite of
escape

COVID and I are Getting Old in Dallas
Deborah L. Bean

On March 23, 2020, Dallas County, Texas, went into lock-down. It was my 64th birthday. When the virus first spread, my husband and I had already isolated ourselves because of our ages and my compromised immune system and diabetes. As well, I suffer from degenerative disk disorder, PTSD, depression, and anxiety, which caused me to become disabled back in 2018. After my 2019 flu shot, I still caught a mutated Flu A in autumn, and bronchitis and Flu B in February, this year. So you can understand how terrified I am of COVID-19.

As news of the big scare disseminated, my husband and I stocked up on food, water, and, yes, toilet paper. We had enough that we were able to give away several packages to other families. Then, my church cancelled all meetings worldwide, even before most cities in the US started quarantining. Before the shutdown, I volunteered one evening a week for my church, but after, I didn't dare come into contact with the people I could be helping. Without that, and my Sunday worship services, I feel isolated.

My husband works from home now. His company sent workers home and told everyone to not come into the office. I hear him on conference calls all the time. From their words, it is obvious people are coping with various trials, such as kids and no home office. From my house all people hear are the dogs barking occasionally or that time when I fell and couldn't get up.

I'm not worried about my husband and me, but I'm really worried about my children. In the early days of the contagion, my daughter was exposed while working on a golf course, by two individuals who later tested positive. Then she and her wife got sick. They'd isolated themselves but couldn't get tested, so they worked on the assumption they had either the milder form of COVID or the regular flu. I wanted to go take care of them, but they demanded I stay away for my own protection. Luckily, they could work from home. Since that time, they've been tested and it came back negative. Now, she's moved to Tucson to help out my mom.

Then there's my son. His family is healthy but he owns a DJ and Karaoke company. He worked six days a week, plus did weddings and other events before the quarantine. His income dropped to zero in one day. He had to let all of his contractors go. And without work, he has no income. He also doesn't have a lot of savings because he does his job out of a love for music, so he's one of the millions of American entertainers with no backup. He's gone to work part-time for a pet store so he has some income to support his wife and mother-in-law.

As you can see, my story isn't horrible or tragic, just the same as for many others out there, worldwide. My husband works; I write, clean the house, and talk on the phone to friends and family; and my husband and I binge-watch the TV. Thank goodness for streaming services, meal delivery, and the fact that my husband and I are close enough that we don't drive each other crazy when stuck together for long periods of time.

Although now, it's months later. I've gotten more depressed. I've put on ten pounds. But we finally received our elliptical machine, over 2 months after we ordered it. The exercise is doing some good for my outlook, even if my weight hasn't dropped yet. We still binge-watch, and talk, and we read – thank heaven for Amazon! We also order groceries curbside, get take-out and prescriptions by drive-thru, and talk. I cuddle with the dogs in the mornings and get some housework done in the afternoons. Plus, now I'm taking a copyediting course.

These are hard times for so many people. At this point, just as things were starting to look better, I worry—with all the partial openings, parties, and rallies going on, and many people not wearing masks—that we are going to go through another upswing in cases and deaths. I know this pandemic is deadly. Last month, a friend's twenty-something nephew died from COVID. We have to get a handle on this virus. I don't believe the propaganda that a vaccine will be ready soon because I understand how science and testing work. So, until a proven solution to this situation becomes available, I'll just stay here, cooped up with my husband and the dogs, until it's safe.

PRIMPING IN QUARANTINE
Madeline Sharples

I spent over an hour today
plucking, shaving, showering,
shampooing, drying, ironing
my hair and lathering my face
and body with lotions
and ointments meant to keep me
moist and youthful.
I then put on clean clothes
carefully picked from all the items
unworn for months
during the Pandemic shutdown.
While I take a last look in my mirror
I wonder what I did all that for.
I'm only going down
to my writing room, sit at my desk,
turn on my computer,
and write this poem. No need to do
any of that other stuff
while in quarantine
to put these words on this page.

REMEMBER ANNE
Jane Gragg Lewis

My life shut down for two weeks in mid-March, 2020. Schools, stores, restaurants, gyms, hair and nail salons, museums, parks and beaches, sports facilities, sports, theaters, Disneyland, the zoos and aquariums, canceled flights and cruises…the list goes on and on. I wondered if I could survive two long weeks of nothing. But I somehow found I could. I counted down the days and was thankful no one could shut down my bike rides. I survived!

And then, Governor Newsom extended the Covid-19 shutdown. I listened to friends, acquaintances, neighbors, people I didn't even know, complain: "I can't get my hair done!" "I need a manicure! A pedicure!" "Oh, how I miss dining out!" "The store is out of rice. Chocolate chips!"

It didn't take long for me to wake up and remember how easy we all have it, and I started making myself very unpopular by telling people they had nothing to complain about, that they were being very petty.

When I start feeling sorry for myself, all I have to do is remember Anne. She is my "go-to girl" when I need to rid my life of self-pity.

Anne Frank and seven others lived in 450 square feet for 761 days. And then it all ended badly—very badly. The world is, always has been, always will be, too full of people who have *real* problems. We should all give thanks that we live in a country like the USA.

I have nothing to complain about. Very few of us do.

Masks

SEWING WITH GOVERNOR CUOMO
Linda C. Wisniewski

My mother sewed all her life, in factories and at home, and all my life I pitied her. She complained about the factory bosses, and fussed over the prom dresses she made for me and my sister in endless uncomfortable fittings, a memory that brings me no joy. And yet, when the Covid epidemic demanded I stay at home to protect my health, I turned to my sewing machine.

I was worried. I never expected it to last this long. In January, when the virus came to the United States, I hoped it would stay in the Pacific Northwest. When my state of Pennsylvania entered a lockdown in March, I thought we'd all stay home for a couple of weeks and it would be over. We learned that facemasks could protect us but we were not to buy them nor to hoard them. There weren't enough for healthcare workers in hospitals and nursing homes. It was a scary time, but women, men, and even teenagers turned on their sewing machines and got to work. When my professional quilter friend Bobbi shared a pattern for masks on Facebook, my distracted brain focused like a laser. Here was something I could do.

A YouTube video showed me how to get the pleats right. Three were best, facing downward so as not to trap particles of virus or dust. Two layers of quilters' cotton was recommended, and I had plenty of fabric in my stash.

My mother taught me to sew on her black Singer when I was a little girl sitting beside her at her bedroom window. My modern Bernina model is much more complicated than that old Singer but it also sits beside a window, in an upstairs room where I write, quilt, and practice yoga. It took a few tries for me to get the cutting and sewing right, but soon I was making masks from my plentiful stash of brightly colored fabric. And still I worried.

For his April birthday, I sent a couple of homemade masks to my younger son, Matt, who lives in New York City, at that time the U.S. epicenter of the pandemic. On one of our video calls, he stepped away from the camera at 7 p.m. to join his neighbors at their windows, clapping for "frontline" workers, in the "trenches," battle terms of the fight for so many lives. When the applause ended, he closed the window on the almost constant sirens of ambulances racing to New York University Langone Hospital, four blocks from his apartment, where refrigerated trailers were used as extra morgues for the overflow of bodies. I said a prayer for his safety, then said another for the people in the ambulances.

New York is my home state, and I've always paid attention to what was happening there. When Governor Andrew Cuomo began his daily press briefings, they became a touchstone for me and millions of others. Every morning, seven days a week, at 11:30 a.m., I logged in on my laptop and sat down at my Bernina. Scissors, fabric, and cutting board at the ready, I cut and sewed masks for friends, nurses, relatives, and anyone who asked because suddenly, everyone needed them.

Women sewers in southeastern Pennsylvania, where I live, started a Facebook group – Mask Makers of Doylestown – that grew to 881 members. One woman set up her front porch as a pick-up and drop-off point, with socially distanced bins for completed masks, cut and uncut fabric and elastic. The masks were donated to community hospitals, nursing homes, and assisted living facilities throughout the Philadelphia area.

On some mornings, Governor Cuomo spoke from Albany, the state capital near Amsterdam, my hometown, a city I knew well, where relatives and friends still live. As the epidemic wore on, he traveled to hospitals with names and in places familiar to me – Buffalo's Roswell Park, Long Island Jewish Medical Center, SUNY Upstate in Syracuse, and a temporary hospital at the Javits Convention Center in Manhattan. He urged New Yorkers to "practice humanity" and be "New York Tough," smart and loving. His folksy, meandering manner and his running jokes reassured me every day.

"Let's start with an indisputable fact," he said at the end of each week. "Today is Saturday." That he could joke after working seven identical days each week, as the weeks ran into each other, assured me that all would be well one day. My sister who lives near Albany said he was not so popular before this crisis.

"I don't care," I said. "He's keeping me sane." I sent her a couple of masks for her trips to the library and her part-time job at Marshall's as soon as the store reopened in June.

My friend picked up a few from my doorstep before her daughter-in-law's night shift at a nursing home. From upstairs, I knocked on the window of my sewing room and we waved at each other, no longer meeting face-to-face. None of us knew who might be infected, and personal contact with all but close family was forbidden. I saw her treat her hands with sanitizer after she got into her car. Later that night, she sent me a photo of her daughter-in-law in scrubs, wearing my mask. Sadly, she got the virus anyway. She recovered, thankfully, and was back at work in a couple of weeks.

I texted Alison, another friend's daughter who had just started her first nursing job at a small Philadelphia hospital. Could she use a mask? Yes! she texted back, and we enacted the pickup scene again, me at my window, she on the sidewalk, blowing me a kiss, raising the bag of masks in one hand. She, too, was infected, before the hospital put mask protocols in place, and was home for 10 days, monitoring her oxygen level and reporting back to her doctor every day by phone. Her mom and dad dropped off cookies and waved at her from the parking lot outside her high-rise apartment. As soon as she was fever free, Alison went back to work. Though still tired, as a new nurse, she would not otherwise be paid.

For 111 consecutive days, including weekends, from March 2nd to June 19th, the governor of New York State remained a voice of sanity in a frightening world. In the audience, chairs far apart, I learned to recognize the backs of reporters' heads and their voices. I knew exactly where the New York Times' guy sat – front row, left side. Each day the governor's message slightly changed. At first it was the lack of adequate ventilators and protective equipment, then the statewide death toll – over 1,000 people a day in mid-April. On March 31, the positivity rate in New York was over fifty percent. After its rapid rise, the curve on his daily chart began its slow downward slide, and my worry eased a bit. This nightmare would end.

By the end of May, I had made and given away 107 masks. The Mask Makers of Doylestown disbanded on May 23rd, having given out 17,390 masks. I stopped sewing but continued watching almost every day as the news improved.

When restrictions were gradually eased and my corner of Pennsylvania reached the "green" phase at the end of June, reality sank in. This was not going to be over for a while. Our local positivity rate was low, but deaths were increasing in the South and West. I thought of my mother, living with uncertainty and fear during WWII. I don't know if she had time to sew back then. But I know this age of anxiety is not new. The women in my family worried and struggled, too. And they went on to see a better day.

On August 20, for the 12th consecutive day, New York's positivity rate was less than one percent.

REFRAMING THE PANDEMIC
Sarah Fine

Let's call it dust
inside the house
where we shelter
vacuum it away and
wet mop the floor
to keep the dirt
down

Buff the furniture
with medical grade cloths
use ecologically correct
wood cleaner
to bring back
the lustre

Inside we can control the dust
Outside that's a different story

Outside the soot rises
and floats
spreads from

the robust activities
of neighbours
settles on the porch
knocks at the windows
insidious searching
for a way inside

Arrives in small gusts
with the daily post
and the take-out dinners
fills the air with distrust
and causes me
to carefully adjust
my common mask
when I go
outside
let's call it dust

MASQUERADING IN A PANDEMIC
Joyce Boatright

I cannot speak for other countries, but masks have become weapons in America's culture and political wars.

Initially, in late February and into March 2020, the public could purchase disposable masks for $30/box of fifty, or about 60 cents apiece. Ours were baby blue, and my husband and I looked like we were playing nurse/doctor. Many folks in our small Texas hometown, however, took issue with scientists and health officials who warned us to mask up or suffer a terrible, life-threatening illness. They thought we were blindly lining up like stupid sheep and yielding our right to wear or not wear whatever the hell we wanted. They rejected donning masks because the masks were uncomfortable, and it was hard to breathe in them. Never mind that hundreds, then thousands, of people were being strapped down in ICUs and hooked up to medical ventilators because they could no longer breathe on their own. They said it was their constitutional right to go mask-less in public and their 2nd amendment right was more precious than your life or mine.

It has become obvious that if we are going to have any success in getting everyone to mask up, we're going to have to change the conversation. Six months into the arrival of COVID-19 in the United States, it appears that is happening—masks have become an economic boon for entrepreneurial cottage industries and corporate big businesses alike.

As America sends it children back to school and adults back to work, selecting a mask is becoming part of the daily ritual of getting dressed.

Here we are in September, and there are masks in solid colors, camouflage, polka dots, stripes, and checks; in animal prints, including leopard, cheetah, tiger, and zebra; in bold designs, such as cartoonish Mick Jagger lips and Salvador Dali mustaches; insects from butterflies to bumblebees; and delicate flowers of all varieties. Companies are expanding their marketing though custom print masks from Starbucks to Gucci.

Of course, when the fashionistas embrace mask wearing, status-climbers will push luxury mask-making to higher stratospheres. An Israel-based jeweler announced last month that the company is creating the world's most expensive face mask, encrusted with 3,600 white and black diamonds and valued at $1.5 million. It's being designed for a billionaire art collector who likes to stand out. Am I being presumptuous to think this billionaire has a Marie Antoinette attitude toward displaced citizens throughout the world who are unemployed and homeless? Louis Vuitton announced in *Vanity Fair* magazine that it is the first to offer a high-fashion face shield, retailing for $961 before sales tax. Evidently status-seekers are eager to show their wealth on their faces, everyone else be damned.

In the meanwhile, college coeds are getting their bling fix by purchasing masks with sparkling rhinestones for less than $20 on Amazon.

A couple of pluses have been discovered in this recent acquisitory behavior. One, since masks cover so much of the face, women are skimping on or skipping altogether their makeup rituals. And as our weather turns colder, masks will also warm our unpainted bare faces.

Secondly, wearing a mask helps introverts avoid the social niceties required when we meet each other face on. Even extroverts and social butterflies feel antisocial on occasion and being masked gives people implicit permission to keep on walking instead of stopping to exchange pleasantries.

As with any new virus, the more we know, the more we realize we don't know. As I write, scientists are beginning to argue about the protection a nonsurgical mask can give us against COVID-19. Most health officials admit it is no panacea.

But here's the thing: wearing a mask during the pandemic provides a *visual reminder* for people to thoroughly wash their hands often and to distance themselves from one another inside buildings, stadiums, malls, subways, trains, buses and other crowded areas. Just as we need caution signs on our highways, we need masks as visuals to remind us to stay safe during these surreal times.

WEAR IT; DON'T CARRY IT
Madeline Sharples

She was walking straight toward me
on the narrow sidewalk
that runs from my house to downtown.
So I veered to the right
into the traffic
to walk around her.
She was wearing her usual
wide-brimmed hat, her red jacket,
loose-fitting sweats,
carrying her drink in one hand
and her mask in the other,
holding it by one
of the behind-the-ear straps.
I take a look at that
and want to scream at her:
why is that mask in your hand
and not on your face,
you selfish person you?
Now I've known this woman
for years – she married
an old boyfriend of mine.
But that doesn't make her infection-free
when she walks by me.
Or anyone else for that matter.

THREE TALES OF MY CALIFORNIA QUARANTINE
Nirmala Kshatriya

It was March 9, 2020. I was lying down, trying to fall asleep, feeling very happy dreaming about reaching my home in India. Both my bags were packed and ready for my flight the next day. I was thinking about getting my house in Bangalore cleaned. This was the house I lived in for nearly 35 years with my late husband and where my three kids were raised. Now the empty house was locked, holding all the memories of my thriving life in its heart.

The morning of March 10, my oldest son called me and said, "Ma, I think you should cancel your tickets." I was puzzled – was he joking? But it seemed he was serious. He said he was concerned about this virus called the Coronavirus that was spreading in China and Europe at that time. At my resistance, he suggested we delay my travel by a month to allow the virus to dissipate.

So, I kept my bags packed, hoping that everything would settle down in a month's time and then it would be safe for me to travel to my home in India. Little did I know that my plan of spending a few blissful months in Bangalore visiting friends and relatives would be replaced by months of quarantine filled with surprises, separations, new forms of connections, unexpected discoveries, simple joys, and a brand new normal.

TALE ONE: THE BABY ON THE SCREEN

In California, I'm accustomed to living with my older son and his family in Los Altos. My youngest son lives close by in Sunnyvale and my eldest daughter also lives close by in Santa Clara, all within ten minutes driving distance of each other.

I loved visiting my youngest son and his wife in Sunnyvale to spend time with their newborn son, my youngest grandchild. There is no equivalent to cuddling with my baby grandson, kissing his curly head, and participating in his excited discovery of the world. His crawling, sitting, babbling and chuckling shone a warming light into my life. I so looked forward to my weekend visits with my young grandson!

I chose to shelter in place with my daughter in Santa Clara, just 4 miles from my grandson. My visits to see him now morphed into excited FaceTime calls that gradually took on an undercurrent of desperation as the months rolled on. I scanned the phone screen for proof that my quickly growing grandson still recognized me, still loved me. His milestones – scooting, crawling, then walking, his first few teeth – were all witnessed on the phone even though I was a mere ten minutes drive away.

In my culture grandmothers have a big hand in raising grandchildren. I traveled to the US from India each time one of my four older grandchildren was born. I helped with the feeding, bathing, cleaning, and performed the requisite Hindu rituals as part of my grandmotherly duties. Being separated for months with no end in sight was quite unbearable and left me feeling adrift. Finally, on Mother's Day, all three of my children and their families gathered for a backyard party. We all sat at a safe social distance. It was wonderful to see all of my children and so odd to not be able to hug them.

My precious youngest grandchild had grown taller in the two months I had not met him. His newly sprouted teeth showed every time he smiled and chuckled. He walked confidently now and toddled about exploring the backyard seeming not to notice me among the throng of adoring uncles, aunts, and cousins. He explored the lawn, negotiated the stairs, examined the wind chimes, then decided to try the snacks laid out on the little table. He picked up a piece of sliced onion and held it up with curiosity. That's when he spied me. He stared at me intently as if jogging his memory, searching where he knew me from. In the next instant his face broke out into a broad smile and he toddled forward with an excited chuckle, holding out the piece of the onion at me like it was a precious gift of love. I cooed at him and he collapsed into my lap still holding out the onion as if to feed me. My heart melted with so many emotions the most precious one being the pure generosity and love of my baby grandson. All my concerns that he had forgotten me in the two months of quarantine fell away at the sight of his bright eyes and babbling face.

The quarantine taught me that the love of family persists – even the love that a young baby holds transcends physical separation. Thanks to modern forms of communication we continue to nurture our bonds. I may have missed my grandson's milestones in person but I was just as present for them on FaceTime. He calls me "Dadi" excitedly when he sees me on the screen, and recently proudly showed me that he has learned to do the Namasté.

Tale Two : As Physical Separation Grows, Virtual Separation Shrinks

A month after canceling my journey, I finally unpacked my suitcases. I put away my clothes and the gifts I packed for my 68-year-old brother and his family, and my friends of more than 40 years in Bangalore. I called and messaged them to say I wouldn't be arriving just yet, I was waiting out the virus. As the days turned to weeks and news of the rapid spread of infections in the US spread all over India, I started to receive messages from family members in remote parts of India who had gotten my phone number from other relatives. They were checking to make sure I was safe in the US. The conversations lead to updates on their families and my family; I got to see pictures of new babies, new brides and grooms, and got updates on graduations and jobs.

The pandemic caused far-flung relatives to get reconnected. My children and I loved updating each other on the happenings of cousins, aunts and uncles. Remember the cousin who was a rebellious 10-year-old? Well now she is an influential leader of a community and a grandma to boot!

As I looked at the gifts that sat in the back of my closet, I realized that the regret of not meeting my family and friends was replaced by the joy of frequent video calls with so many precious relatives – a connection that would not have happened if not for the pandemic. In a time of forced isolation I found my calendar packed with warm connections with my extended family, some of them long forgotten but so loved.

Tale Three: Protecting Our New Soldiers

When my children were little, I loved to sew cute outfits for them. My daughter's frocks with their elaborate smocking, buttons, embroidery, collars and sleeves were the talk of the town. I made pageboy collars on soft masculine prints for my young sons' shirts, with embroidery on the pockets of trucks, bears, giraffes, and lions. My daughter now shares my enthusiasm for sewing and has a trusty old sewing machine in her house.

When I read about doctors and nurses putting their safety on the line in these dire circumstances, I was shocked. There was very little known about the virus in March other than that it was highly contagious, the symptoms were very uncomfortable, and the mortality rate was high. On top of all this, there was a shortage of Personal Protective

Equipment for the very people who were treating patients afflicted by this contagious virus! It felt as if our precious healthcare workers were soldiers out in a war zone without suitable protection.

When a friend in Los Altos asked for help to sew masks for healthcare workers I immediately volunteered. I sewed over fifty masks out of HEPA filters. The dining table was covered with material, elastic, and thread for a week and my sewing machine whirred incessantly.

The City of Los Altos recognized my efforts by writing a volunteer showcase on me. It was a sweet gesture but the effort of sewing the masks was more valuable to me in a couple of ways. It allowed me to contribute to the safety of the healthcare workers, and took my mind off the sadness of my canceled trip to India.

MEDITATION, MAY 2020
Ariela Zucker

I remember a lone rock overlooking the vast panorama of the Judean desert. It was one of my favorite places when I needed to gain perspective. The last time I sat there was a late afternoon in January of 1991. That night operation Desert Shield, or in its formal name, the First Gulf War, began.

For weeks we were bombarded with warnings and speculations about the possibility of a chemical attack. What it meant we couldn't even fathom, but the fear was real and all-encompassing. The constant warnings and daily government guidelines controlled all our waking moments and penetrated our sleepless nights. Life as we knew it – was it about to end?

The list of what we needed to do to protect our lives and those depending on us was endless. Masks against toxic air filtration, plastic sheets to cover windows, pails of water, and rugs to be placed under doors. It did not make much sense, I know it now, but the experts supported it. Fear, it turns out, is a strong incentive.

That rock in the desert – we used to call it the end of the world (such irony). I sat there by myself, I thought of my family in our house up the street: my husband and my daughters. I looked at the desert, savoring the quiet. For a moment I could pretend that things were not going to change.

The sky was lucid blue, the desert as always, a bit secretive and full of beauty. The setting sun painted the otherwise dull brown palette in shades of orange and gold. The round hills went on and on, till they fell into the Dead Sea, a splash of blue on the horizon.

We came to Arad – a small town balanced on the edge of a cliff, and the last spot on a narrow meandering road – to immerse in the quiet. But now that the world was upon us, all I wanted was for it to remain whole. For things to stay as they were. All the complaints and dissatisfaction faded away, became insignificant and trifling.

Please, God. I prayed, as I never did before. *Make my world stay whole.*

Two months later, normal life resumed, and soon it became obvious that most of the guidelines were completely misguided, if not outright damaging.

———

These past weeks I checked on the world, again on the verge of losing itself, from my kitchen window. *Shelter in place*, this new term that took hold so quickly and made my physical world small and clearly defined.

If not for an occasional person with a dog, the neighborhood appeared deserted. It reminded me of the scenes one can see in apocalyptic movies, when the hero (perhaps heroine) walks into a once vibrant city, and there is no one in sight.

My kitchen window gave me the best view of the surrounding streets. Several times a day I watched over the houses around and hunted the streets for signs of life. At night I took comfort in the lights I could see in the windows of my neighbors, and the weak illumination of the streetlights.

"We are in it together," the TV and radio kept bombarding the audience day and night. Guidelines and instructions showered by serious looking scientists backed by statistics of the growing toll. I held on to my tiny corner of sanity. It was not much, one small neighborhood in the center of a town that is not famous for much.

In the back of my mind an old soundtrack, almost forgotten, cracked and coughed back to life. Twenty-nine years have gone by, but the recordings were familiar, and their effect so well known. Fear of the unknown will make a person do almost everything – as illogical as it might appear during normal times.

I knew, standing by my kitchen window, that while part of the whole, if I want to keep my world intact, I should trust my common sense. I've seen it before and remember how easy it is to put a mask over one's eyes and call it protection.

CHEMICAL FALL
Christina M. Wells

The soft soap in the hall bathroom smells like chemical fall. It's the artificial smell of October and November, and it doesn't generate images of pumpkins, apple cider, fall sweaters, or multi-color leaves, swaying over roads on the way to country restaurants and wineries. Or maybe it does, sort of, or I wouldn't have thought of all of those things just now. The bottom line is, something about it feels saccharin, like an artificial celebration of what we'd all rather be experiencing in person.

There's something off base this morning. I woke half-leaning out of bed, my head too close to my cell phone as the alarm rang. My face felt flushed, the familiar heat rising. There's central heat and air, plus a ceiling fan, and I'm (usually) cold, except when I'm not. There's something odd about hot flashes. In them we are hot, though not really, and there's a kind of mixed reality. My feet can be cold, but suddenly the heat rises through me. I'm left with the thought that I'm feeling something no one else is feeling, though hot flashes are way too mainstream to be as otherworldly as we make them out to be, when we're the one having them.

My wife Jen picked out her clothes for the day, and nothing in them suggested the kind of heat that I'm experiencing. I suppose there's the alternate heat we could prepare for, the August heat outside our front door. There's no point, really, since one of us may step outside on the deck with the dog, or I may go out for coffee (for her) and matcha (for me). These aren't big enough excursions for us to acknowledge the outside world. Instead, we prepare for another day of working from home.

There's something odd about the ad I get that reminds me I've signed up for a course on trauma. I've signed up for a course on trauma during a pandemic. On some level, we all could offer up something for the instructors. We could also all easily say that we haven't signed up for a course on trauma, and we're getting one, whether we've signed up or not.

I slipped a filter in a mask when I walked out the door, and I wondered, at least a little, when I touched the door on the coffee place and walked across the tape designed to separate one customer from another.

It is not as though trauma is new. One of the trauma conference speakers will talk about military service, and one of my most vivid memories of teaching is a student telling me about hiding in the basement of her home while bombs went off overhead. When we think we've invented trauma, it's with that next level feeling that on top of whatever else we've experienced or heard, there's this – the thing keeping us inside, or making us think we are daft for even bothering to go out, climb into the car, and exhibit the audacity to go somewhere, anywhere.

Still, when I look out the window, I don't see trauma. I know it's there, in the stories students shared with me, friends share with me, and family share (or don't share) with me. I know it's inside me, whether hot or cold or medium. Or buried. And even right now, with this icing trauma, this trauma on top of whatever other kind of trauma, things are bright and alive. A tiger swallowtail butterfly maneuvers over the neighbors' new flowers. A man walks slowly but confidently in the distance, not like he's running for his car, his house, his life.

I think about opening my laptop to add the dates to my calendar, the ones for the trauma conference. Discussions of trauma are still things we can schedule. We are in control. A shiny set of smiling faces appear in the ad, the experts who can say, yes, yes, we are happy pandemic programming, though we help people see more clearly the things that are neither clear nor happy.

There's so much that we can learn in a pandemic. I can buy a contemporary satire of academe though I've quit teaching, and I can sign up for a book group to talk about it with people associated with the library where I researched when I worked on my doctorate, years ago.

I can virtually shop at an area bookstore, and I can ride by and pick up books with a bottle of wine from their wine bar. That's something I haven't done yet.

There are probably an infinite number of places where I could take yoga, and if I sleep through East Coast yoga, I could easily sign on for West Coast yoga. Maybe I could even take it with colleagues from the coaching school I attended. Their headquarters are on the west coast.

I could sign up for mindfulness meditation with one of its western leaders, and I could switch to TM meditation later in the day, in the time specified for my time zone, or even my city, specifically. Perhaps there would be something novel about meditating at my computer, knowing the meditation place, if it's really open and not someone's living room, is right down the block from the White House. Trauma. Real, national trauma, not theoretical trauma. Not buried trauma, either. It's pretty much right there, on the surface.

I have Zoomed and FaceTimed and video-chatted and texted, like so many of us who have played connect the dots—and squares—with friends, family, colleagues. I have also decided, at the end of a writing day, to do a free quiz on tarot, plus a virtual reading.

I have joined writing communities, spaces to network and learn and share. Take that, agents of the world, there are all these middle-aged and older people here, and some young, all of whom would buy each other's books. We all *do* have platforms, we do.

I have thought of going to a film festival that I always intended to go to on the ground, with one or another of our friends who live near the place where it normally takes place. There, I might get to see things that feature women and racial and ethnic minorities, and LGBTQIA+, and old people, and all the people who often get left out when we see things in person. I could have seen them in person once, before we had this pandemic. But the point is that I can't, and the movie distributors often didn't put them where I could see them anyway. Now I can see them, though I can't leave the house. I can see them though a lot of people still won't, because they are online doing something else.

I have downloaded Zoom backgrounds, some of them for the places I'd rather be when I'm sick of working in the guest room. We can play pretend. It's easier to deal with trauma when New Zealand is behind us, especially since their prime minister's policies made it possible for them to leave the house. None of them are working remotely, with the smell of chemical fall, their own chemical fall rushing over them while they put up a fake background behind them. It could almost be spring.

There is still serendipity, even in trauma, in a class or not. I just got an email from a coffee place, telling me I can download more virtual spaces for my chats and meetings. I can pretend I am at one of their stores, and I can tell all my friends, hey, let's meet with the same storefront behind us.

None of this felt real in the beginning, and pretty much everyone said so. Now it feels real, like acceptance, or at least like the kind of trauma you deal with on a schedule, especially if your insurance covers that sort of thing. It feels real while everything around it is fake, reminding you that some heat really is from summer, or at least from global warming. Not everything is your temperature rising while everyone says it's cool. Not everything is a season experienced once before, or behind you on a screen. Some of it is real, real, real, no matter how much we mask it, call it a trauma course, and put it up as a fake wall behind us.

MASKS
Jeanne Baker Guy

It was July 18, 2020. I awoke to the news that John Lewis had died from pancreatic cancer. Tom Perez, chair of the Democratic National Committee, said in tribute, "Last night, Congressman John Lewis passed away at eighty years old, leaving behind a legacy of activism and service that will echo for generations to come. His zeal for justice was only matched by his capacity for compassion."

Perez went on to say, "Congressman Lewis never failed to remind us of our moral obligation towards one another. He lived his life acting on behalf of those facing injustice and oppression and then encouraged us to do the same—from the streets of Selma to the halls of Congress. In a moment where we have been driven apart, in a nation that feels as divided as it has ever been, let us allow John Lewis to bring us together one more time. Allow his memory to continue to lead us toward that more perfect union."

And how do we find, how do we create, a more perfect union?

This morning's early brisk walk took me to the Veterans Memorial Park a few streets over from my house, where I momentarily and bravely (yes, bravely) donned my mask. It normally remains tucked at the top of my exercise pants, but for the first time, my daily walk in this COVID world required masking, not once, but twice.

Four people of color, two men, two women, one couple masked, the other not, were in a pensive conversation and did not immediately move over on the wide path close to the monument to allow for social distancing. It didn't appear to be out of disrespect; they were unaware of my approach. As I put on my mask, I thought of my new writing friend's recent haibun (a literary form combining prose and haiku) entitled "Only Connect," a masterfully written, deeply moving piece about human interaction in today's sad, masked world.

When I was in close proximity to the two couples, I said a good morning, which was returned in kind, and they compassionately glided to the side.

Later, a middle-aged non-masked Hispanic woman and I approached each other on a narrow stretch of sidewalk. I put my mask on again and as we slipped past one another wished her a good morning. Unsmiling, she seemed lost in thought and surprised by my greeting. I think she mumbled a quiet hello.

I'm purposely identifying my nonwhite COVID-world friends because I am so painfully aware of my whiteness with or without my mask. Masked, my brown eyes speak for me. I want my eyes to say hello and good morning and enjoy the day and I'm grateful for your presence. It's almost as if I want to hide my whiteness so I can see and be seen as a fellow human.

What does it take to create that more perfect union? Connection. Masked or not, it is our moral obligation to keep our eyes and our hearts open. With every chance afforded us, large or small, comfortable or uncomfortable, connection is critical. Our future depends on it.

Fears

PANDEMIC EYES
Betty McCreary

The first time I wore a disposable mask into a store was in early March. I hated it. I couldn't breathe and my breath stank and I felt hot. A few more shopping trips and I got used to wearing one in public. I was being safe and doing my duty to protect others. Not everyone wore one and I stared at them and moved away. I had begun to enjoy my anonymity. I stopped bothering with makeup and the state of my hair I excused as pandemic related.

One thing I did not get used to was the bare grocery store shelves. In mid-March I ventured out to a nearby grocery store. There were too many empty shelves. I had seen some the week before, but thought those were anomalies. The bread shelves held no bread. There was no milk at all in the dairy case. There was no cheese. My daughter, back from college to do online classes, had requested ramen. The shelf that usually was filled with ramen was bare. The frozen pizza area was picked almost to the bone. I walked around the store in awe. I did buy a few items, but the only things on my grocery list that I actually found were wine and toothpaste. Driving out of the parking lot, I started to cry and was pretty blue the rest of the day. We were lucky that we had food at home and at least no one we knew had gotten sick.

By April, so many in person events were being cancelled. Our grandson's first visit to Texas, scheduled for mid-April, was cancelled. Family member's trips abroad were cancelled. My husband and daughter and I began to celebrate family birthdays drive-by style. We would drive to the person's house and park across the street. Wearing party hats and holding up a Happy Birthday banner we would sing the birthday song with our masks on. I attended two children's birthday parties virtually via Zoom. One was for a grandniece turning seven. One of her little friends told her how she wished she could play with her and give her a birthday hug.

As frustrating as the social distancing became, there were good things happening, too. I got to enjoy an impromptu street dance party that a couple of moms had for their children. The kids lived across the street from each other, but could not play together, so one mom set up a sound system. The kids and the moms danced and laughed, safely apart, yet together. A stranger in a parking lot kindly offered me some extra disposable gloves. I got to see the Air Force Thunderbirds fly over Austin to honor the frontline doctors and nurses and others. My writing groups started meeting via Zoom. We wrote out our frustrations and feelings about the pandemic, racial relations, police brutality, and the growing street protests.

By June my old fears were returning. The fear of the marketplace used to be an individual neurosis and felt familiar to me. As a child, I used to be so anxious and shy around people I didn't know well, that I would not speak. Through years of therapy and life experience I had claimed my voice. I became a person who could greet strangers at the store or church. But now, I am once again the introvert. I feel anxious as soon as I leave the house to head to the store. I am watching more TV now. I yell at the actors for not social distancing, something I would never do in the real world for fear that some anti-masker would cough on me. One day I slipped and fell hard on the tile floor in my dining room. Even before I landed on my hip and arm, I prayed that no bones would get broken. I did not want to go to a hospital because I knew they were filled with the covid-19 virus and over stressed workers.

It is August now. Sitting in my car, I observe the people in the parking lot. Some don't put on their masks until they are at the store entrance. Others put on their masks before they get out of their cars. That is what I do. I turn off the ignition, grab my purse and car keys and put my mask on. I position it properly with both mouth and nose covered. In the store, I peer over my mask at the other shoppers, making sure we don't get closer than six feet from each other, which is often not possible. Do I have to wait until the person looking at every brand and type of soup finishes or can I hold my breath and pass them in the narrow aisle? I never really enjoyed shopping for food. Now, I hate it. At least there is more food on the shelves.

I want to stop whining. I know I am lucky. So many people have gotten ill and too many have died. As time has gone by, I now have friends and family that have gotten ill with the virus. I don't know anyone who has died, yet. I am grateful for the technology that keeps us connected to our sister and brother humans, but I want to be able to look directly into someone's eyes. And I am tired of looking at my own face on the computer screen.

I get some peace in being outdoors and enjoying nature, but even the shapes of certain flowers or seed heads remind me of pictures I have seen of the spiky covid-19 virus. Every part of life now seems to be filtered through the lens of the pandemic. If you had told me a year ago that we would all be wearing masks, I would not have believed you. I wonder what our country, and the rest of the world, will be like a year from now?

PRAYER FOR MY PANDEMIC MIND
Jeanne Baker Guy

Based on a conversation about poet and theologian Pádraig Ó Tuama and his definition of prayer. Prayer is, in part: rhythm, comfort, disappointments, words and shapes, all feelings, desires named.

I ask to be
seen and heard
and accepted
for whoever I am,
for whatever I'm feeling at this
   moment in time,
allowing me to be with the
   naming
of ALL my feelings and fears

Remove the pressures,
self-induced or otherwise
The Fitbit wants 169 more steps
Let me go
for just two hours, please

Let the naming begin
and let my heart break open to
much needed self-compassion

Let it be what it is
Let me be okay with it, whatever
   it is
Let me not stop caring
Let me not have to go to the
   grocery store today
Can't it wait just a few more days?

I need time to breathe
and be silent
and feel my fears
all the way down to my bones
where my mind
cannot play tricks on me

Let me
see
and feel
and not be afraid or too weak to
   do so

WHO'S UNDERNEATH
C. V. Shaw

I stood still, as people in yellow medical gowns ran around me. Half their heads covered in sky blue. Their eyes, dispirited, peered at me for a second then darted away. Emotional numbness seeped its way into my cells. Only the sound of my shallow breathing into what looked like a white cardboard bra cup with a minuscule vent was familiar and comforting to me. My breath was all I had. It now identified me. As without it, I, Janet Bloom would cease to exist.

I didn't need to see their lips move to know what they were saying to each other. I could see how the exhaustion in their already tired eyes stole the last bit of sparkle when they looked my way.

"Another one," I was sure that's what they were broadcasting to each other with their looks. No words necessary. I was just another number to add to the statistics, another risk factor for them, for the city, for the world.

I bent my knees slowly allowing my bottom to kiss and slowly melt onto the navy blue plastic chair. It had been a really long time since I had done anything for myself. This had become my me-time. Awkwardly, it felt good. For a minute, I forgot I had three elementary school-aged kids. I was now forced to relinquish any mom or wife duties. It felt good to not feel guilty over it. I started to remember me.

"Huh, the silver linings of COVID," I thought to myself.

Normally, I would have called Carl, my husband, to check on the kids and read a tutorial of when and how to handle their daily activities – today I wouldn't. He called on my drive down to NYC Presbyterian Hospital and I didn't pick up. I read his text when I parked, asking if we had extra batteries for our bedroom TV remote. And here I had been thinking he was calling to check up on me.

"Figure it out yourself, you little pompous self-righteous son of a…*bat!*" I whispered assertively to my phone as I threw it in the messy black pouch I call a purse. I knew he was pissed because his mother, Shirley with her burgundy helmet hair and her red lipstick, was not allowed to leave her house for the safety of her old ass, so he was on his own.

"Bloom!" called the nurse draped in baby hues of yellow and blue holding a clipboard.

I stood up quickly. Maybe too quickly, as my head throbbed and the waiting room spun around. I grabbed the back of the chair for support, pinching my fingers between the wall and the ridge of the chair.

"Dammit!" I dropped right back into the seat.

The nurse, stiff as a statue, just stared at me. I took as deep a breath as possible and slowly came to standing. I took another breath and followed her into a busy hallway.

"Sit there," she said, pointing her finger wrapped in blue latex at a rolling desk chair they had obviously confiscated from one of the offices, due to the overwhelm of patients.

She held the thermometer and stared at me for a few seconds as if she was waiting on something. I stared back into her tired, large, exotic brown eyes. It was the only part of her that wasn't covered. "Philippine? Indian?" I asked myself, trying to find some type of humanness about her. Had she not spoken, she could have literally been a short man for all I knew. I felt sad not seeing the rest of the person, the physical attributes which make them different than the rest.

"The eyes are the windows to the soul. What if we could only see people's eyes and connect only with their souls," I started imagining. She suddenly spoke loudly past the facemask.

"Your hair. Move you hair!"

Quickly, I swam out of the depth of this existential ocean I had fallen into.

"Sorry," I said, as I pulled my brown dirty strands behind my right ear. She adjusted a giant clip softly squeezing my left thumb, and simultaneously prodded the tip of the thermometer in my ear. It quickly beeped. She discarded the disposable tip announcing my temperature, "101.9."

She stood stoic, entering information into the laptop that sat on a rolling cart. I tried to scan her employee badge for a name and a picture, still searching for a human under all that medical apparel.

My body suddenly became chilled. I shivered and tried to stop myself from coughing several times for fear of infecting her.

"Can I please have a blanket, I'm freezing."

She walked away, quickly returning with a blanket and handing it to me. She looked at me and took back the blanket, opening it up and draping it around my back. She patted my back. I had not felt someone care for me in a long time. My eyes watered as sorrow woke in my heart. The chatter of life had not let me hear the sadness that had become me.

She prodded my ear again. "102.6. O$_2$ decreasing 74," she called out to the heavy-set male nurse across from her.

I wasn't afraid of death, and right now it felt more enticing than going back home. I had never contemplated suicide. It was never an option. I had been a good Christian. This wouldn't be suicide. This would be death by COVID.

"May I please use the bathroom?" I asked the nurse.

She pointed to a door halfway down the hall.

I grabbed my black pouch and slowly headed down the hall and outside the hospital to my car. I reclined my seat and found a comfortable position, imagining the peace I would finally find when my lungs, like me, gave up.

I heard a tap on the window.

"Mrs. Bloom, you gotta come back."

I sat up. "No! Please walk away."

Silently she stared into my soul and I at hers.

A STORY, IN REVERSE
Laura Maurer Goodell, MD

and when it's my time to go,
    know that I love you.

and when I'm in the ICU,
    if there isn't a window, paint a mural of the sky and a tree,
    once a day, play loud dance music, because why should everything
        be so sad?
    then play Iz's "Somewhere over the Rainbow,"
    tell me the date and the time, remind me where I am,
    have photos of me everywhere to remind them that yes, I am a
        person,
    walk me, stand me up, move my legs, so if I recover, I'll be able to
        walk again,
    please talk to me, and tell me you love me.

and when I go to the hospital,
    tell the doctors and nurses to take good care of me,
    ask for a window room, but at least let me have a plant,
    put a big bowl of chocolates in my room, so they'll want to check
        on me,
    let me bring my security blanket or a stuffed animal,
    plaster the walls with photos of you,
    please call me and tell me you love me.

but for now, I will prepare, I will get ready,
    I'll make my body as strong as I can,
    by losing weight, because we all know that besides age, obesity is
        the risk factor
    I will walk the dog outside in nature, enjoying the sunshine on my
        face,
    and I will connect with friends, and family,
    every day I'll savor warm lemon water with a teaspoon of local
        honey,
    I'll run and twist and bend,
    and I will dance in the moonlight,
    I'll take slow deep breaths through my nose, while I can,
    I'll try to give you all my wisdom but realize you have your own,
    and I'll tell you I love you.

PRAYER
Catherine Johnson

It was a cool, gray, late April morning, but the cherry trees along the road were full of petal-pink blossoms that flurried in the slightest breeze. I was on my way to pick up a friend for her chemotherapy treatment in the city. It would be the first time I had left the island in 8 weeks. The first time I had driven with anyone else in my car. And even though spring had faithfully arrived, my heart felt wrapped in the stillness of winter.

    I arrived at my friend's house, mask on, promptly at 6:30 AM; plenty of time for us to catch the 7:00 ferry. After exchanging pleasantries, we drove in silence. My friend didn't feel much like talking. Neither did I. We were both feeling anxious.

As April COVID cases soared in Seattle, our rural island of 10,000 residents remained strangely untouched. We only had 4 reported cases, 1 hospitalization, and no deaths. And while masks were not yet required, they were already highly visible in our community. My friend had offered to find another driver for this appointment, someone younger, less at risk, but I had agreed to this date back in February, and when I say I will do something, I follow through. Now, as we drove to the ferry, I wasn't so sure. My decision to leave the island for the city, for a hospital no less, felt like a decision to enter a minefield. *Please keep us safe,* I prayed as we drove onto the boat.

In late March, our Governor had ordered a "shelter in place" mandate, as a result Seattle was deserted, the freeways nearly empty. My friend and I drove from the ferry terminal to the hospital in record time, parked for free on the street where shops and restaurants were closed and boarded, like a scene from a post-apocalyptic movie. We entered the hospital, our temperatures were taken, and we answered the requisite questions: no cough, no respiratory symptoms, no known contact with anyone testing positive for COVID-19. The nurse placed a yellow paper band around our wrists, a sign that we had been screened, and we soberly proceeded up to the infusion center.

All morning, I was religious about wiping my hands. Whenever I opened doors, or pushed elevator buttons, I used an alcohol soaked hankie, which I kept in a zip-lock bag in my pocket to clean them. I also routinely used the bathroom and gave those two good hands yet another wash with lots of soapy suds. I wore my mask the whole time, which wasn't as bad as I thought it would be, five hours of mask wearing. I kept social distance as best I was able, stepping back and out of the way for others to pass. For the most part it was easy, except in the infusion room, which isn't a room at all, but rather a 9'x9' space with curtains separating it from the other spaces on either side, and the nurses' station behind. In each "room" there is also a computer, an instrument cart, IV stand, reclining infusion chair, and one more chair for people like me: a family member, a driver, or a friend. All of this, and us, in 18 square feet of space. When it was just my friend and I, we were probably within range of the appropriate six feet of distance. But whenever the nurse came in, which she did every 30 minutes, she had to thread her way between my friend's feet hanging off the end of her infusion chair, and me, tucking my 34-inch inseam legs ever tighter against mine. I looked like a frightened contortionist, but consoled my worried self by thinking: *at least we are all wearing masks.*

After three hours of sitting quietly, talking with my friend, listening to the constant pumps and wheezes, beeps and pings of chemo machines, I'd had enough. I needed real air. I excused myself, went downstairs and out of the building for a walk.

A few blocks from the hospital stands one of Seattle's most magnificent Cathedrals, Saint James. I had heard that many Catholic churches, closed for regular services, were still open during the day for private prayer. Saint James was no exception; "Open from 8:00 AM until Noon – daily," the sign on the massive door read. It was around 11:30 when I opened it and stepped inside.

I hadn't been in church since the middle of February and I sorely missed the sanctuary I find there. As I entered the dimly lit interior of the church, I could feel myself beginning to relax and release a tension that I didn't realize I had been holding, maybe for months. In a small alcove to my left stood a carved wooden statue of the Virgin Mary, surrounded by a hundred, pencil-thin tapers burning steadily. Tears started streaming down my face. I felt so tender, so touched. It was as if I were greeting my own mother, who has been dead for almost 20 years. How I wished for her voice, her reassurance, her embrace. Was I longing for my Mom, or for our Blessed Virgin? I don't know. Either would help, both would be great; the thought caused me to smile even through my tears. I lit a candle, made my prayer and waited, listening, still crying, still longing for reassurance.

Eventually, I made my way to a pew in the main part of the church. I noticed that there were a handful of others scattered about, heads bowed, praying in the stained-glass shadows. By now my tears had wetted my mask and the collar of my shirt. *Where are you God? Please help us, help us all.* Then something in me quieted, I stopped asking, stopped listening so hard for answers, and just gazed at the altar bathed in light. A private peace spread through me, a peace in which I could rest.

On the far side of the church, a young woman appeared and started moving quietly from person to person, notifying each, with only a gesture, that it was time to leave. Because I was on the opposite side, the side closest to the door, I would be the last asked to go. I had a little more time.

The altar in Saint James Cathedral sits in its center and is made of gleaming white marble. It is positioned beneath a large domed skylight from which the day's brilliance pours in. It provided a stark and beautiful contrast to the rest of the darkened interior. I could not take my eyes off that streaming shaft of light.

Slowly, one by one, the others began filing past. Each paused at the altar, bowed their heads in reverence, and then walked quietly out the door. It struck me that there was something unusual about this solemn parade. Gradually it dawned on me; every one of the passing petitioners was attired the same. Every single person wore medical scrubs. Some still had their stethoscopes draped over their shoulders. I was the only person in the Cathedral that morning wearing street clothes, the only person who was not a frontline worker caring for others in this deadly time. I thought my heart would break. *Please God, keep them safe.* My tears began all over again.

What is prayer, really? A plea, an unanswerable "why," a whispered gratitude, an empty silent longing that bears no name? The young woman finally reached me and motioned for me to go. I was the only person left. I nodded and stood. But as I turned towards the door, I glanced back at the altar one more time. My gaze traveled up, following the light into the glass dome overhead. There I saw an inscription painted on the ceiling surrounding it. From my angle of vision, I could only read a portion of it, but it was the one I most needed. It said simply: *"...I am in you."*

Please keep them safe anyway, I murmured, and stepped back out into the day.

THANK YOU, MR. ROGERS
Teri Liptak

The dusty-pink scarf was cool and silky beneath my fingers. A whimsical pattern of miniature perfume bottles and lipstick cases decorated the fabric. The day I found the expensive scarf on sale, I had imagined the many ways I could wear it. Folded over my mouth and nose, held onto my ears with yellow ponytail holders was not one of them. Yet, after watching a You-Tube tutorial, I was doing just that before going to the store to stock up on essentials.

I walked around the house to get a feel for my makeshift mask. It was surprisingly secure. Our dachshund gave me side-eye as I passed her, and seemed quite nervous. The cats, however, ignored me. It would take more than my resemblance to a fashionable Billy the Kid to rattle them.

An hour ago, a National Emergency due to COVID-19 was declared. The experts in pandemics suggested wearing face coverings along with social distancing when in public. There were rumors of a coming "lockdown" and a shortage of cleaning supplies and toilet paper. Toilet paper? Seemed crazy. Still, it nudged me into action. Who wants to be the one who gambled and ran out of two-ply? I jotted down a quick shopping list for the week and grabbed my keys.

In the Wal-Mart parking lot, I struggled to get a pair of latex gloves onto my clammy hands. Adrenalin flooded my body as I scooped up my purse and opened the car door. My normal routine of shopping for my family, which I usually enjoyed, now felt like I was Rambo on a mission. Sweat popped out on my brow. No one else was wearing a mask.

Much like a deer's nose twitches to pick up the scent of danger, my body hummed with uneasiness once inside the store. Every uncovered face felt like a threat. It seemed like an ordinary day for the other shoppers. Some looked at me as if I were crazy.

Mean thoughts ricocheted through my mind as I shopped among these reckless strangers. I wondered which person might get me sick with this bizarre virus. Would it be the silver-haired woman in the Mrs. Roper-style caftan talking loudly about her bursitis in the vitamin aisle? Perhaps it would be the barrel-shaped gentleman rubbing his eyes by the eggs and butter.

"Just keep your distance from everyone, and you'll be fine. You can do this," I told myself. It became my mantra as I idled a safe distance behind others and pretended to study my list as I waited my turn at the shelves.

Things were going as good as they could with my strategic six-feet apart buggy maneuvers, when it happened. No one else was in the pet food aisle, and I let my guard down as I filled the buggy with Friskies and Greenies.

"I don't know anything about cats, but a stray showed up. I guess I should get some food. He appears to be sticking around." The husky voice was loud and close. Too close. I could have lifted my elbow and touched the woman reaching over my head for a bag of Meow Mix. I felt my cheeks flush with white-hot anger at her intrusion into my space. It made me even more aware of the ridiculous mask on my face and the lack of one on hers.

She smiled and waited for a response. For some reason, this made me angrier. I wanted to scream at her. Instead, I glared at her as I jerked my buggy away. A look of confusion flickered on her face, and her smile died. Good, I thought as I stomped off. Hopefully, my abruptness taught her something. Don't crowd a stranger during a pandemic. I fumed about the clueless woman all the way home.

Later that afternoon, still brooding over the incident, I sorted dirty clothes in the laundry room. As I gazed out the window, a brilliant flash of red caught my eye. Beneath the low-slung gray sky, along the equally gray road beside our house, toddled a small girl in a fire-engine-red sweater. A "Schindler's List" moment. She was flanked by a man and woman I assumed were her parents.

The man and woman wore face coverings, and the woman carried what looked like a black bandana in her hand. I imagined the mother trying to keep it on her daughter without much luck. Some battles with toddlers, you just couldn't win. I felt a kinship with her as I recalled how difficult it was to keep any head covering on my now-grown son when he was little. In his pudgy little hands, winter hats and tiny baseball caps had all become frisbees for me to chase.

The girl plucked a bedraggled dandelion from the weedy roadside and handed it to the woman. The woman took the offered treasure and hugged the child. As I watched these parents doing their best to maintain a sense of normalcy for their toddler, my mood softened. The tender scene comforted me on a day that had felt alien and dangerous. How hard it must be to raise a little one during this strange, awful time, with everyday life now on shifting ground. Watching them renewed my reverence and gratitude for family bonds and human connection.

I realized I had to steady myself to experience life in an unpredictable way. How do you bring two worlds together? The one you knew and loved, and the unfamiliar one you must come to accept?

My thoughts turned to how I had treated the woman at Wal-Mart earlier. On a regular day, as an animal lover, I would have gladly shared advice about cats with her. In that moment, I had chosen fear over kindness. I had withheld my compassion and denied her a sense of companionship during a stressful time. What if she didn't have anyone to talk to but a random stranger in the store?

Your actions become who you are, and this wasn't the person I wished to be. Shame washed over me.

Even at fifty-one years old, I am a work in progress. Life is not lived in a straight line. Over and over again, I go back to the beginning. I must own the dark part of my nature. In Buddhism, there is a powerful quote: "If you focus on the hurt, you will continue to suffer. If you focus on the lesson, you will continue to grow." I must allow myself to be fully human and then do better.

———

Days of self-isolation blend seamlessly into months, and COVID-19 is still prevalent. There are many people who are not taking precautions. I'm still scared and frustrated. However, I can't live in a state of emergency forever. Like it or not, there is uncertainty in life. As Natalie Goldberg stated, it was time to "build a tolerance for what you cannot bear." Time for the unnatural to become normal.

Some walls have gone up, but others have come down as this pandemic lingers. I watched footage of a zombie-like woman licking the window of a closed bar in a deranged protest and others screaming at store employees when asked to wear a mask. My faith in humanity and goodwill towards others dwindled. Then, I remembered the child dressed in bright red on that dreary day and the intense emotions she stirred in me. The lesson reveals itself.

Even during this "in-between time," there is a need for connection. I can't pause my life and wait until this crisis passes. As Fred Rogers said, "Look for the helpers." This is a perfect time for those wise words. Not everyone is being irresponsible. Most want to do the right thing. I need to try to stay open and compassionate even in an unsettled world. Especially in an unsettled world.

I don't want the frame of my life built on fear and frustration, but instead, on gratitude and kindness. The energy I put out into the world matters, if only to myself. During this uncontrollable time, the one thing I can control is how I treat others. Extending kindness is not always easy, but it's always worthwhile. I choose to be a helper.

QUIET IN THE TIME OF CORONA
Susan D. Corbin

The quiet of the lockdown
In an older couple's home is
Shattered by the small dog
Doing her duty

She protects them

From the roar
Of the lawnmower next door
With barks as loud
As the sounds they protest

From the couple walking
Hand-in-hand down the street
Outside the window
Too close to her territory

From the UPS guy
Valiantly delivering packages
Of brightly colored creativity
And knocking on the door

From the next-door children's
Screams and shrill shouts
While running outside
In the sunshine with siblings

It is a full time job
Shielding the humans
From such dangers.

She does it well

SICK DAY
Christina M. Wells

Yesterday I took the day off for the first time since quitting my job. There's a line if I ever heard one.

I was sick during the pandemic, though not WITH the pandemic. When I woke up, I had this immediate feeling of sinus pressure, a pressure headache with possible swelling on one side of my face. Had I still taught for the college, I probably would have gone down to the kitchen, opened a drawer, taken some over the counter stuff, and gone. Maybe I would have done that had I been teaching from home, as I did in the latter half of the spring term.

But I looked outside at the gray and the rain, the clouds passing overhead while my head felt like it might explode. I got right back in bed, curling up to see if/when the headache would pass.

It was strange when I woke up congested and cradling my head. I've had sinus headaches for at least the past twenty-five of my forty-six years, yet my first impulse was to tell my wife, "IT'S NOT COVID!" I decided not to contact one of my two best friends, the one who had used her own antiseptic and sheets when she and her husband went to a cabin for the weekend.

Later, when I felt better and fielded a text message from my mother, I followed up "I'm sick" with "not with COVID." I did the same thing with the best friend who DIDN'T take antiseptic on vacation. I told her this even though she went to a beach with a small pod of friends, and I didn't see masks in the pictures.

When my head stopped hurting so much, I listened to some cello music while I half napped. I knew the day would come—the day when I would be sick with something while the pandemic was happening. At least it was something obvious, the kind of thing I might have powered through until I got old enough to know better.

The surprising thing, though, is that illnesses need qualifiers, somehow. In the span of a life, maybe especially at midlife or beyond, we can think of many things that have gone wrong, and many absolutely wrong things that are actually normal. It's odd to think that a pandemic we've only known about since earlier this year would give us a reason to say, "Yes. I'm sick with something, but not something like that."

Beyond that, guilt over a sick day rises up when the illness is such a nothing compared to a contemporary plague, or any number of medical conditions that might make one worse. How hard would it be to walk across the hall, open my Scrivener software, and get to work on the manuscript I've got going? It's been so easy to write this book, at least so far, maybe because of the extreme situation that there's nowhere to go, really. Two concerts we intended to go to were canceled, and there are no plays or musicals or movies. Even though some restaurants have indoor seating, we aren't the people sitting there.

We've been to two Virginia wineries where we could sit outdoors, spaced far from other patrons. But for the most part, we've taken the dog to doggie daycare (I saw that eyeroll), and we've run basic errands. We've gone for rides, until the point where I realize I have to pee and we go home.

All of this is to say, I really can work constantly, most of the time, though lately in the evening, we've saved some time for Rachel Maddow on MSNBC and *General Hospital* from earlier in the day or week (yes, an astonishing and unlikely combo). I've also felt like we've needed evenings and weekends, especially since for sixteen years, I taught full time at a college and incessantly graded.

But in bed, in pajamas, with my head nearly exploding, I thought—sick day? I could crawl across the hall and sit with one of the cats, developing a business plan for the coaching and editing business I haven't yet formally started. I could read something that could qualify as research. I could read a memoir I just bought, for instance, and I could say it's about studying the narrative arc, or some such nonsense. I could work. I could meta work.

But I couldn't, and for every slight conversation I had that day, I had to say, "But it's not that bad, really." If it's not COVID, and it's not cancer...how could it be that bad? In a weird sort of way, that crosses my mind, even though the headache gets to be its own thing that comes and goes.

Once in my doctoral program, I went to see a famous, charming British professor, and because I hadn't wanted to reschedule and I needed approval for a paper topic, I had worn my hair draped over one side of my face, one that was swollen from a sinus headache almost to the point of disfigurement. "I might miss class later," I said, pulling back my hair. "*Oh dear God*," he said, his accent getting more pronounced with every one of the three syllables. I can't for the life of me think of why I thought I couldn't reschedule. He was reasonable. He was even appalled.

Maybe the memory of that headache is embedded in me somewhere, swelling and all. There's something in me that thinks I should go, go, go. It could always be worse, so much worse, in fact, that if I get a text, if the phone rings, if an email comes in, I feel like I have to say something. It's not COVID. It's not COVID. It's not COVID. Part of this is admittedly because I'm a pretty neurotic person, and many people in my life are prone to worry, too. But part of it is the comparison. This will pass, and in a day or so, I'll be fine. I probably won't even see a doctor. I should want to tuck this away somewhere and get on with the show.

I remember being small and stuck at home in pajamas, with my bright yellow walls and *Wizard of Oz* wall hanging. My dad came home with comic books for me and asked me how I was, smiling. For whatever reason, I remember feeling guilt. And for what? That I didn't go to a stimulating, enriching day of first grade? Where did that come from, that feeling I had done something wrong and would need to tell someone?

I remember eighth grade, when my periods were already so bad, so awful. I sat in my dirty, gray science room, the one set up right next to the room where shop classes were held. There was lots of action there, and we in science were low-key in comparison. I remember a girl stretched out over her desk, moaning, saying something about cramps to the teacher, a man. He looked at her and said, "Well, you can go home, but if you stay here, you're going to have to sit up and listen." Sit up and listen? There was no way, no way. But it was said like an admonishment, like leaving would somehow be the weak way out.

Somehow a sick day feels like that, especially when my commute is so short that I can walk it without any shoes. It's not only that I don't want others to worry. It's also that things have been made so convenient. I mean, I work for myself now. Hello. Somehow that makes it worse. I am not even pulling out the laptop, logging into a system to ask for leave. I'm having to judge based on totally internal criteria, whether or not I can take the day. And I should.

On my mom's side, a cousin's husband had COVID, and maybe one of their kids did, too. He definitely had something, before his dad did. On my dad's side, a cousin and his wife both have COVID.

Who knows how long this will go on, and what kind of symptoms will linger? I had a headache. I may get another thinking about it. This time, I feel I have to keep going, as if we aren't all having a gigantic sick day, one we've worked through for months and months.

Lest We Forget
Joyce Boatright

Coronavirus
continues its killing spree;
politics be damned.

Parenting

LITTLE BY LITTLE
Julie Chavez

It's a Wednesday morning in September of 2020. I sit in bed, still in my pajamas, pillows propped up behind me. The puffy white duvet is smoothed over my legs and my laptop sits open on top of it. I'm viewing a virtual version of Back-to-School Night, flipping through slides and watching presentations uploaded to YouTube. I'm trying to ground myself, trying to accept that my children's distanced learning will remain as it is for a while, and that they won't be going back to school anytime soon.

My husband, Mando, and I toasted the New Year with the rest of the world on January 1. The kids wore glasses in the shape of the year: 2020. We loved the roundness of it, the way the year seemed to roll off the tongue sounding balanced and bouncy. Mando and I clinked our glasses of champagne against each other and said *I love you* and *Happy New Year*, but we infused those words with our tender hope, let the words carry our unspoken, shared wish to each other: *Let this be a good year.*

We couldn't have known that our hopes would be crushed underneath the steamroller that has been 2020. We couldn't have known that on this Wednesday, we'd be living through a pandemic in the midst of a brutal political climate while California's second largest wildfire rages just to the south of us, pumping smoke into an orange sky that can only be described as post-apocalyptic.

I've just finished arguing with my youngest son, Eli, about having one of his social-bubble friends over to the house. The question, "Can Kole come over and work on our stuff for Block class?" incited a half-hour of debate about having a friend over in the morning, about whether they'd actually accomplish anything, about how the visit would impact the day's Zoom schedule and would Kole stay for the call and would that impact our Wi-Fi. After a few rounds we were tired of bickering and I told Eli that Kole could come over before the Zoom call but I wanted him to leave before it began. It was a frustrating, confusing conversation and its conclusion left us both unsatisfied. I went into my room with my laptop and my mug of tea to try to rescue the morning.

Now, I take a quick sip and place it on the nightstand before I click on another video. This video is for my eldest son's eighth-grade engineering class and I see the face of his teacher pop up on the screen. She's dynamic, passionate, and she appreciates these gawky, awkward middle-schoolers. In the video, she discusses the laser cutter she acquired last year; she says she hopes they'll be back in the classroom to use it.

In a year that's packed with loss—ambiguous and definable, tiny and massive—it's that sentence that breaks me this morning. It's the thought of that fancy, brand-new laser cutter sitting in an empty classroom gathering dust, unused by my son or any other children. This small, sad vision is enough to crack my shell, and all the larger sadness of this year rushes in through the sliver of space. My children are safe and they'll be fine and of course the laser cutter is a ridiculous luxury. But what about the kids who might have their lives changed by a teacher like this one, by the wonderful teachers in so many schools? What about all the children who are falling through the cracks in our country, who aren't safe at home, whose circumstances have now shifted from less-than-ideal to desperate?

I work in our elementary school library, and when I went in yesterday I found a parade of ants marching across the circulation desk. I crushed them one by one with my thumb as I thought about all the kids who *need* to march into the library every week, who need this small safe haven. I squished five ants before admitting defeat. There are probably thousands of ants I can't see and they'll just keep coming, the little bastards.

The sum is more than the parts: the ants and the laser cutter and the loss and fear and suspicion at every turn, so much joy canceled in a calendar year. I set aside my laptop and slide my legs up under the comforter so I'm sitting cross-legged. I set my elbows on my knees and place my head in my hands. I weep.

Mando walks into the room; he needs no explanation as to why I'm losing my shit on the bed because, well, it's 2020. He walks over and sets his hand on my shoulder as I say, in between the sobs, "It's too heavy."

He squeezes my shoulder and says, "I know," because we're well past any pep talks, having exhausted those reserves in April or May. This year is a dumpster fire and there's no end in sight.

He speaks gently, "Come on. Let's eat breakfast."

I briefly lean into him as I take a deep breath and wipe the tears from my eyes. "Okay," I agree.

We walk out of the bedroom into our short, narrow hallway and run into Eli and Kole. I'm still crying, still in my pajamas, but thankfully I'm wearing a bra. I look up at the boys and say, "Good morning, Kole. I'm just having a little breakdown. Has your mom cried recently?" Kole's mom is Katie, and she teaches fourth grade at my school.

"Nah," he replies. "But she said everyone else on her team has cried, so she's surprised she hasn't yet." He shrugs casually and I laugh at these matter-of-fact words uttered from a bony eleven-year-old.

"Good for her," I say sincerely, shaking my head. We walk past each other in the hallway. Kole and Eli disappear into his room and Mando begins to make breakfast. I text Katie to tell her Kole has just seen me crying in my pajamas.

After being treated for depression in 2018, I learned the details matter: if our lives spin out from the center, then we must take excellent care of that core, knowing that the magnification of these small choices increases as they spin out to the edge of the wheel. So when I eat breakfast, I'm sure to drink enough water. I take my vitamins. But the best thing I've done this morning is cry on the bed. It's okay to be overwhelmed, to argue with my eleven-year-old, to say to Mando, *This all feels like far more than I can bear.*

I text Katie, who calls me a few minutes later. We laugh at the absurdity of my moment with her son and we validate and encourage each other in the only way we can manage.

"Katie, I hate everything."

"I know. Me, too."

After Katie's call, I talk to Eli. "Bud, I'm sorry about this morning. I hate doing school this way and I don't always know what the best thing is." Eli is a social bird and it grieves me to see his wings clipped so viciously. "But on another note, I think Kole really enjoyed seeing me crying in my pajamas."

He smiles and says sarcastically, "Yeah, he did."

Little by little: it's how I'm getting through this year, and it's how I'll get through my life.

The beauty in living this way is that I move slowly enough to appreciate the tiny gifts that make life wonderful, even in a year like

2020: intimacy, joy, a good book, a funny movie. I move slowly enough to remember that it doesn't have to be perfect to be beautiful.

In a year when every day feels like its own infinite source of joy and grief, I've stopped looking for the "new normal," stopped waiting for life to achieve some sort of stasis, and it's freed me from the disappointment that this jalopy keeps breaking down. Little by little, I'm making my way down the road, coaxing the engine to life for a short distance only to have it fail again. But when the engine smokes, I pull over and see what there is to do in that moment: read a book or gaze at the sky or pick a flower on the side of the road. I can wait for the engine to cool down.

Little by little, I'll still cover the distance.

QUARANTINE K-POP
Christine Ristaino

As the world slows to a screeching silence, my daughter and I dance. No graduation for her, only a ceremonious grab of this wrinkled 53-year-old hand. She teaches me to move my hips like teenage girls. She grooves with young blood, her body not aware of how flexible and sensual it is. Her every cell dances, united in the purpose of K-pop. There are moments when we stop, sit on the floor like schoolgirls, and laugh, those full-body laughs that sometimes turn to tears. My body no longer moves like hers. My attempts at K-pop are awkward, staccato, clownlike. My daughter is patient. She doesn't give up on me. "Now mamma, you can do it," she says in a mellifluous voice. She shows me each move, over and over again, explains how in numerous ways, and when I succeed, at least in a way suitable for moms, her eyes really do sparkle soft blue. She holds my wrinkled hands, with such warmth, with such hope, that sometimes I want to cry. This is what it means to heal from hardship, from long-ago violence, when an old touch, so unwanted, is replaced by sheer, nurturing K-pop.

OVERHEARD DURING THE 2020 PANDEMIC
Laura Maurer Goodell, MD

"Don't fall off your bike and crack your head open. We don't want to have to go to the ER."

"What's the difference between curbside and delivery?"

"On Friday night, let's get a drive-through frozen margarita!"

"Do you think graduation will be outdoor or virtual?"

"Which will come first? Hair salons will open, or I will actually care how my hair looks."

"Does watching YouTube count as homeschooling?"

"I know we've already walked four times today, but let's go for another walk!"

"If I'm eating all these home-cooked meals, why aren't I losing more weight?"

"Can you put chlorine in a six foot blow up pool?"

"You make me so mad!"

"I love you so much."

DAYCARE IS DIFFERENT NOW
Christina M. Wells

Sometimes we have gotten in terrible traffic on the way to pick up our son after work, the kind where I wonder if we'll be one of the last few cars to arrive. I silently think of those parents as slightly negligent, though I know people get held up in meetings, lose track of time, and get caught behind accidents on 395. They have busy lives we couldn't possibly know. Besides, my father forgot me twice when I was in elementary school, and I haven't held onto that my whole life. Hmm.

Lately, there hasn't been traffic on the way to daycare in the evening. We breeze by the shopping mall with the bagel place, the Japanese restaurant, and the Trader Joe's. We head by the movie theater, or what is normally the movie theater, when we aren't having a pandemic. There's a gym, and there's a small storefront that sells Peruvian chicken. There are a few historic signs tucked away, saying things about the Civil War and its aftermath. But mostly there is no rush hour, so we don't notice much but the lush trees and the church with the funny signs out front, and when we get near the daycare, we pull up our masks so that we're ready for the people who staff the pick-up lane, the same lane that functions as a kind of kiss-and-ride in the morning, sort of like at the DC area metro stations.

It's one of the schools that decided to stay open, and we're lucky that way. It's decorated in a calming purple, with a sign up celebrating seasonal holidays in the front room, along with pictures of well-lit classrooms and happy students, hamming for the cameras. And if a parent is anxious, or simply having a bad day, the staff is amenable to the parent stopping by to see their kid in the middle of the day. I've never done that, not so far, but a close friend I taught with has gone by. Let's face it, none of us would trust a school that minded parents showing up suddenly.

We've also learned that because our son has advanced rapidly, he's been placed in the same classroom with our friend's son, who is older. There's comfort in that, especially at a point when elections, the pandemic, and an assortment of uncertainties loom. We look forward to seeing their class pictures together. It's a sign that something is normal, that not everything is in Zoom squares and email distribution lists.

No wonderful place is perfect, to be sure. We've learned that a few people call our son "Beef" because his name is Angus. When we named him, we were thinking English, Irish, and Scottish heritage, not cows. I suppose no name is everything. We had thought about Seamus because some friends have a son with a friend named Seamus, and we like it. That seems like a cute name on someone small, but I kept imagining people saying Sea-muss. I thought we had done better with Angus, but he is good-natured about the nickname, and the teachers have been good at understanding why we don't want this nickname to stick.

One of my friends asked me recently what Angus had done wrong to get sent to daycare at a time when both his parents are at home working. I suppose that's a fair comment. When I sit at my desk and write, I sometimes see small children outside on bicycles, presumably taking a break from homeschooling. Older kids go by with their backpacks, slowly shuffling their feet, and a teenager walks every day around the same time, so regularly that I notice when he's late.

But maybe we should be on a quest for something normal right now, something like a routine. We have to work, even if it's at home, and kids have to go to school, even when it's at home. Plus, Angus is very social—he loves running around with his friends. A staff member at daycare conspiratorially told us that Angus has a girlfriend named Ava. He's not even three yet, so this is all very sweet. But maybe that's one reason he's so quick to run out the door, on a good day. He's got friends like Leo and Harper and Linus. And he's got Ava.

He also got put in a special athletics class, and he certainly didn't get that from me. It's on Thursdays, and we get a separate report card for it. There are pictures and sometimes videos that are emailed, and he looks so striking, balancing on bars and running on the blue mats. It's really all we need to explain to our friends why Angus goes to school right now.

Sometimes he does trudge out of the house in the morning, sleepy and discontent. He'll pull back a bit on the front sidewalk, just in front of the hanging flowerbed. Perhaps he thinks if he throws a tantrum in the stretch between the front door and the car, he'll get to stay home. It's like he knows that we're all home right now, and let's face it, how could he not know? He only goes to daycare a few days a week, and sometimes when we pick him up, we're wearing our weekend pants. Who wouldn't notice weekend pants, after seeing all the parents show up in suits?

Once he gets to daycare, he's happy to be there. He goes bounding in the front door, looking for his friends. Maybe he's even looking for Ava. Then, when he leaves, he drags a little sometimes, like there was one more game that needed to be played, and we interrupted. It's embarrassing, really, how badly he wants to stay. But we're told that a lot of the others do the same thing. Still, I'm happy when I know that the afternoon staff was there in the morning, looking at how much he wanted to hang out with us all day.

Besides, when he stays home, he's tempted to curl up on the sofa and sleep. The cats are sleeping, and we're working in makeshift offices in the dining room and the spare room. Who can blame him for wanting to be like the ones who are sleeping? I've even noticed his bizarre grooming habits, something he obviously didn't pick up from us. "Angus, you're not a cat," I say to him. And he looks up with his warm, forgiving brown eyes, as if to say, "No shit. But since I am a secure collie mix, I'm going to let that go."

I suppose that it could come off as a bit weird, taking a dog to daycare during COVID, and to some, it might come off as funny to take a dog to daycare on an ordinary day. But he's a bit like our baby, and who wouldn't want their baby to have a more normal life than they are having? Sometimes the trips to drop him off and pick him up are the only trips out during the day. In between times, we are expected to work, pay bills, and not think too much about the relatives who have had COVID, or the friends and family who might, later on.

We do have a social conscience, and for that reason, it's actually sometimes better to skip the news. On those days, we go out in the backyard with the dog, watching him run a course through the bushes, over some rocks, and up to a tree where a squirrel dangles himself overhead, in jest. But some days, when life gets too serious, we buckle Angus in the back of the car instead, and we drive through Northern Virginia, where he can look out the windows at the world, or he can nestle his head down and sleep through whatever's happening outside. Then, when he's really bored and wants to run, we can take him to his friends, while we wish we could see ours. Whatever happens in the world that day, we'll have his furry face on the other side of it, happy to see us in pants that can get muddy, headed back toward home.

Love

HOME RANGE: FINDING HEART AND HOME
IN A PANDEMIC
Susan J. Tweit

When COVID-19 upended all our lives, I was six months into a new relationship with a man I had met in Wyoming the fall before. When his dog introduced us at the guest ranch where I was teaching, we had both been single for the better part of the decade and neither of us was really looking for a partner. No matter. One look at the Guy, from his well-worn cowboy hat and stubby ponytail to his nicely fitted jeans and dusty cowboy boots, and my heart plopped at his feet.

"Dammit!" I said to myself. "I am not interested in risking love again." Besides, he lived in western Colorado; I had just settled in New Mexico. We were hours apart. And yet...

We both felt the buzz of attraction. Only we were working, so we didn't really have a chance to get to know each other. After that week, we went separate ways: I headed north to Yellowstone National Park to finish my summer's invasive-plant work, and he and the dog and his four horses headed south to Colorado, where he was preparing to hunt bighorn sheep in the wilderness.

On weekends, when he came to town to resupply, and I was within cell range, we indulged in long phone conversations. One of those centered on the question of what "home" meant. The exchange was sparked by something I had said in my seminar: home for me is wherever big sagebrush grows in the Rocky Mountain region. The "seas" of this aromatic shrub that fill valleys and basins throughout the region, I explained, map my place in the West.

"No sheep died," he said, when he called at the end of three weeks, "but I had an interesting realization."

"What was that?" I asked from Santa Fe.

He described hiking uphill through open ponderosa pine forest, the dappled light of aspen groves, into the high-elevation Douglas-fir and spruce forest, and then the widely spaced groves of bristlecone pine, before emerging above treeline in the windswept expanse of the alpine, with its turf of plants no more than a few inches tall.

"I realized that I'm not comfortable in the alpine," he said. "It's not my place. It's too exposed." Where he felt at home, he said, was the forests and woodlands, and the sagebrush country. "I realized that my home range could be described by that of dusky grouse in the Rockies."

While he talked, I looked up a range map for dusky grouse. It outlined a wide swath from Canada to northern New Mexico, a near overlap of the region I call home.

We considered the way the part of the West we both call home coincided, and discussed how we each felt drawn to the whole swath, rather than one particular place. "Maybe for people like us," I said, "home is not a single location, but a whole area. 'Home range,' instead of home. A range to migrate through over the seasons, rather than a fixed spot."

He was quiet, thinking. "I like that idea," he responded. "The way people once moved in search of food and shelter, occupying a whole region instead of settling in one place."

"Exactly!" I answered. "For you and me, home range could extend from the high desert in northern New Mexico in winter to Wyoming in summer."

The Guy came to visit a week later, and by the time he left, we had decided that he and the dog and the horses would come south to spend the winter with me. They arrived after Christmas. Once we all settled in, we spent part of each day exploring the high desert landscape on foot and horseback, and working at the delicate process of interweaving two separate lives—sometimes gracefully and sometimes crashing headlong into each other's tender spots.

Then the pandemic hit. As stay-at-home orders radically transformed life, the Guy became visibly nervous. He wasn't so much worried about COVID-19—my house is outside Santa Fe, with a comfortable distance between the nearest neighbors and us—he was concerned about running out of hay for the horses. And the need to return to the farm to prep his fields for spring and lay out irrigation pipes.

When he and the dog and the horses headed north, I felt bereft. My rural house with its view of distant mountain ranges, spectacular sunsets, and coyotes hunting ground squirrels right outside my sunroom windows suddenly felt isolated. No longer a sanctuary but a lonely cell, where I spent my days in solitary confinement. *Where is home now?* I wondered.

A month later, I sneaked out of my still-quarantined state, and made a run for the Guy's farm. I plunged into irrigating the hayfields, controlling invasive weeds, pruning shrubs and trees in the yard, and other chores. Farm work is inherently socially distanced: our pod was me and the Guy and the dog; the horses, mule deer, swallows and magpies; plus several hundreds of thousands of brome and bluegrass plants. The pandemic seemed far away.

Except on our occasional trips to town for food and farm supplies, when we wore facemasks and practiced social distancing. In his sprawling rural county, with fewer than 20,000 human residents, crowding is not an issue.

Our workdays ran from before dawn until after dusk, leaving us no time or energy to fret about the changes in the larger world. It was oddly soothing to be too worn out at the end of each day to obsess over the grim news.

Then came summer, when I would normally migrate to Yellowstone National Park at the northern end of my home range, and the Guy, the dog, and the horses would migrate to the guest ranch in the Wind River Mountains where we met. Because of the pandemic, Yellowstone was on restrictions and my invasive-weed work was on hold.

When the ranch opened with a reduced schedule and smaller guest capacity, the Guy suggested I join him there. So when irrigation chores slowed down, I headed to Wyoming and spent several weeks surveying weeds and writing up a management plan for the ranch. And then returned to the farm to work, before finishing summer at the ranch with a wilderness pack trip with the Guy and our herd.

The ten-hour solo drive between the farm in rural western Colorado and the ranch in the mountains of northwest Wyoming gave me plenty of "windshield time" to consider how my definition of home has changed as a result of the pandemic and this new relationship. "Home" is no longer as simple as my scientific mind would like, a matter of drawing a tidy line around where big sagebrush dominates the landscape and plopping myself down somewhere within it. Now home includes a messier and less easily definite territory of the heart, including the Guy, the dog, and his four horses.

That realization has—somewhat paradoxically—kept me grounded through these tumultuous times. It's still true that home for me is the range of landscapes and communities between northwest Wyoming and northern New Mexico. It's also true that whether or not I am with the Guy and our four-leggeds, we are connected by the heart and by our shared bond with this part of the West. The challenges we face now are as much internal as external as we navigate the new world of belonging to each other.

My understanding of home is richer: it is the earth beneath my feet, this growing relationship, the weeds I work with, the human community, this changing world. It is the territory I nurture with my whole heart, the life I seed, the world I am part of. Home, however we define it, is where we belong, where we take refuge, who we love, what we stand for. In these times, knowing and cherishing home could be what saves us.

A Flash in the Pan:
A Sunday Morning Argument
Marian L. Beaman

Five large eggs sat happily agitating in the boiling water on the shiny black, glass stovetop. It was Sunday morning, the first Sunday of our state's shutdown due to the Corona-Virus pandemic. It felt odd not preparing to go to church to teach my 2-year-old preschoolers and attend the worship service that followed with my husband Cliff.

Nevertheless, I was determined to make the best of it. "Why not make a hot breakfast for Cliff? Surely, I have the time," I mused. Already, eggs being hard-boiled for later pickling in brine had just begun to boil. While the water was still piping hot, I could surprise my husband. "How about I make you a soft boiled egg? It'll be simple to add another egg to the pot."

"Well, okay, that would be nice." Freshened and shaved, my husband smiled weakly as he ambled into the kitchen, expecting to prepare his usual breakfast of cereal and fruit. Pleased to help, I plopped the fresh egg into the water – one just for him.

"It'll be done in a little over three minutes," I chirped. "Watch the clock. It'll be 8:42 when the egg can come out." As Cliff waited and watched, he popped a slice of fresh sourdough bread into the red toaster.

Walking into the bedroom close by to put on my robe, I could hear the egg skittering around on the plate as he spooned it from the pot, just in the nick of time. As I arrived back in the kitchen, he was assembling a napkin, fork and butter knife to crack the egg. After putting his steaming cup of coffee on the bamboo tray, he shuffled away into his studio to eat breakfast. I'm a morning person, fired up to greet the day; Cliff takes longer to waken and show signs of alertness. Still, I could tell he appreciated the gesture, especially unexpected on a day when the whole world had suddenly stopped.

I could picture my husband enjoying his egg breakfast, the bright sun slating in from the east, cheering his corner studio. Four years ago, when we transitioned to this house, I visualized how my artist husband Cliff could create more art work in this space, like the painting of five swans swimming in a lake under a big rainbow, an image at odds with the blow-up in the kitchen that I didn't know was about to erupt in our usually happy household.

Back in the kitchen, I met Cliff with his empty tray. Wearing a broad smile, I knew I had done something nice for him at the start of a strange day. "How was the egg?" I asked jubilantly.

"Well, it tasted fine, but it wasn't quite done," he muttered.

Disappointed and deflated, in a flash I could picture the yellow-orange egg dripping over the toast, the white of the egg still in its puberty. I could imagine my husband twirling the knife around the inside of the shell, releasing the clear, gelatinous egg white. I had failed! This was proof! Instantly, I flipped from mild disappointment to full-on anger. "You always criticize me!" I yelled menacingly. With that, I stomped, Gestapo-like, to our bedroom, slamming the door.

The global ghost, the Corona-Virus pandemic, had just gripped our nation and the world. Whisperings that had begun in China, and then spread to Italy, were beginning to create waves of terror in our own country. As I recall my blow-up, I realize now that the invasion of the virus into our lives may have triggered the stages of grief, at least for me. And it has occurred to me that I had probably hit Stage 2, anger, just a few days after the crisis registered in my psyche.

Though the emotional temperature in the house had plummeted to near freezing, in the bedroom, I stewed, "I must have lit a firecracker." Feeling offended by Cliff's negative reaction but also instantly angry at my short fuse, I remained in the bedroom to nurse my hurt feelings.

"What will happen next?" I wondered, after I had time to gather my thoughts. Too irritated to confront Cliff right away, I pondered, "Who will make the first move?"

After several minutes of brooding, I ventured back into the kitchen. There was my husband, possibly trying a different tack to restore harmony.

Cliff was grinning near the counter, a nonstick pan in his hand. He had grabbed two steak knives, laying them in opposing directions. Apparently, he had raided cosmetics on my vanity, too: between the two knives was a tube of lipstick, its scarlet cylinder swiveled open. "Here, if we're going to have a duel, you pick the weapon!"

I stood uncomprehending at first, blinking at this odd display of two knives and a lipstick in the pan. And then I got it: Duel or duet? The tension eased, Cliff laughed, and I laughed, too. Holding the pan with one hand, he pulled me toward him with the other hand and we hugged.

"Clever idea. Clever," I said, smiling with relief.

Our "flash in the pan" was a clash, contentious, but over quickly. It was likely a consequence of my reckoning with the fear of the unknown, which the onset of the Corona Virus had injected into our lives, personally and as a nation. The pandemic will have dramatic effects upon all of our lives, as a family and as a nation, for years to come.

However, as a couple in a long marriage, we have learned to recognize signs of discord and look for a remedy as quickly as possible. Like the dictionary of idioms affirms, our tiff was a transient occurrence with no long-term effect. Thank God for a husband who has learned to solve our marital problems in a creative way. Next time, it may be my chance to be the creative duel diffuser! But every time, I hope I'll choose romance over a ruckus.

LOVE IN THE TIME OF CORONA
Susan D. Corbin

You find out who you really love
in the middle of a pandemic
and who loves you.

Who calls you to find out
how you are doing?
Whom do you call?

I called Aunt Agnes, Dad's little sister
whom I have not seen in years.
The joy in her voice was uplifting.

A friend I would not have named as
close, phoned me.
I hope my joy at her call carried to her.

———

Can you live with a spouse
under 24/7 house arrest
ahem, stay-at-home orders?

What I meant…, says one.
I'm sorry I misunderstood, says the other,
please forgive me.

———

Someone said
love is not a feeling,
it is a doing.

WORD OF HONOR
B. Lynn Goodwin

In March 2020, I realize I cannot draw a deep breath. Something is pushing into my lungs—pushing hard. Their balloon-like expansion is gone. Instead, my breath slams into a combination of wet cement and burning coals. My lungs are trapped. They can't tunnel their way out.

Breathing hard, I tell my husband, "I have it," as he walks into our bedroom. He comes towards me and I put up a hand. "Six feet away." He shakes his head. I'm gasping, and there's nothing he can do to help.

This thing that must be COVID is pushing harder and crushing my breathing apparatus. I roll over onto my stomach. Sometimes that moves things around inside. The whole thing came on so fast and furiously that I don't know what else to do.

"Call the Advice Nurse," my husband says.

Like I have my phone.

Like I could move my arm to get it and punch in the number if it were next to me.

This pain is slamming into both sides as if they are no more than skin on a drum. This thing is a killer, just like the news reports said. Infection rates and death tolls informed me COVID wasn't a hoax. Common sense told me not to swallow bleach as an antidote. I assumed it would hit different people in dissimilar ways, but this rapid shutdown is unexpected.

My husband and I are both at high risk because of our age and underlying conditions. That's why I'd been so careful to isolate myself—except for trips to the grocery store, the pharmacy, and the USPS. Whenever I went out, I wore a mask, which is mandated in California. It made sense. What if I was a carrier and didn't even know it?

Though scientists are seeking a vaccine, we don't have all the facts yet. Obviously, COVID is highly contagious, but do we know all the ways it can be transmitted? Isn't it still showing us how it spreads?

"You just won't do it, will you," my husband says, when I don't pick up the phone and call our health care provider.

The pain is pressing in from my back and my sides. It's practically paralyzing me. "Not. Right. Now." A minute later I add, "It hurts too much."

"That's why you need to call . . ."

I tune him out.

Next thing I know, I'm turning onto my side, inch by inch. My joints ache, but that's from fibromyalgia. The wet cement and burning coals have dissipated. Soreness remains. I call out, "I'm okay. Maybe it was gas."

Five months pass. It's August, and the psychological toll is now stronger than the physical one—at least on me. We're healthy and grateful for all that's right in our lives So what if it's 102 degrees in Boomtown, Nevada, where we've parked our RV? We have air-conditioning. My husby gets restless, and we hadn't been anywhere since the quarantine started. I understand and reluctantly agree to go away. I pick my battles, and there are fires raging all over California.

When I wake up Sunday morning, he's fixing breakfast and the 1980s movie *Nine to Five* is playing. How it takes me back. The office has fluorescent lighting. The women wear skirts and heels to work and use their wits to combat the forces of chauvinism.

I first saw that movie in a theatre forty years ago. The movie theatres are closed now. Back then I rooted for these women who plotted against the boss. Back then I was unmarried.

The world has moved forward and I'm married to a man with some old fashioned values. I pick my battles and root for women who go after what they are entitled to. My feminist side has mellowed with age, but it's also endured.

When we hear the harnessed boss in *Nine to Five* say, "Untie me. I won't call the police. I give you my word of honor," my husby says, "That man doesn't know what honor is."

How true! I love his insight.

Sipping my first cup of coffee, I realize that since we married, I have a fuller understanding about the importance of my own word of honor. Today it is one of the few things I still control regardless of the restrictions 2020 has placed on our lives. When either my husby or I give our word, it means something. Neither COVID nor aging can take that away.

Loss

WAITING
D Ferrara

We can't say the words: you are dying, before our eyes, on cameras we placed in your room, and we can't be with you. When Dad died, we were there, waiting for him to wake up (he didn't), waiting for a last word (there weren't any). All we knew is that the only thing he cared about in the days before he lost his words was you. *Take care of Grace. Take care of her.* Instructions about the proper tax treatment of assets – code words for "have I done enough? Have I forgotten anything?"

Your "babies" – why aren't we there? The care home has been on lockdown since mid-February. We can't visit.

Now, in April, we sit in our homes, apart from each other, quarantined. The coronavirus plays out on the news constantly. Constantly, I am angry with those who shrug, "If I catch it, I catch it." How dare they? Their careless behavior puts us all at risk. They party on Florida beaches, go to food courts in Oklahoma, and it all funnels to us, to here. We can't sit with our dying mother because they have to have popcorn shrimp and margaritas.

What would I tell you, if this were a normal Friday, a normal day, one in which I rode my bike over to your home, took you for a walk, sat and watched the sky, commenting on the colors? I don't know – it wouldn't be important. I wouldn't share my fear with you, my concern for our family, our town, the world.

Today, they say I can visit you. I don't want to think about what this means. There is no question that I must be the one who visits. Lisa's chronic cough has damaged her lungs. Ginny is too fragile. It must be me.

Alison, the receptionist, lets me in, directs me to wash my hands. I count to thirty because all the catchy little songs that we've been learning escape me. She hands me a crisp white lab coat, a mask and gloves. She offers me goggles. I turn them down.

It is eerily quiet. The television in the main room is off. There are no games in the dining room, and no food, either. Allison takes me to the elevator, presses the codes. I reach the third floor – the "memory unit."

Your door is ajar. You lie on your bed, pale, but breathing. You have a shiner worthy of a saloon brawler, and bruises down your left arm, from a fall last night. I touch you gently, but you jump, startled. "Mom, it's me. Donna." You don't smile, but you rasp out my name.

I can't stop myself from kissing you through the mask. I want to hug you and only stop because I think I will hurt you. I fumble for the iPad, to continue with the plan... The plan. It was to Skype everyone. Everyone? I am not even sure who that is.

I make the first call to my sisters. You see them, reach for the faces on the screen, gasp, "my babies." We, three middle-aged women, fight tears. I tell you what's on the screen and repeat what is said. The connection is terrible and breaks off. I stab at the screen, pull off my glove. *The hell with it.*

You rasp, "help me" and my heart sinks. I remember my father-in-law, Simon, and Dad, both rasping, "Help me, take me home," as they were wired into their hospital beds.

But no, you want me to help you sit up. You want to see better. I pull you up. It doesn't matter that I am holding you next to me, my mask to your cheek. No distance at all between us.

We try again to talk to Lisa and Ginny. It's a little better, but clearly, we can't call "everyone." We all say, "Love you," and I call my daughter, Brigitte. Your voice rises at the sound of her voice. Shakily, you place your hand on the screen and whisper her name over and over.

We lose that call, too. A bit frantically, I call your other granddaughter, Liz, who is at home with your namesake, five-year-old Grace. Liz and Grace are beautiful, both bloomingly young. Grace tells you she loves you. You say it, too.

I begin to worry that you are too tired to do this, that your mind has wandered to somewhere that I don't exist. Like the days in which you asked politely, "Who are you?" laughing when I said I was your daughter.

I needn't have worried. You know me today, as if my aging face has finally become part of your present. You know your daughters, grandchildren, great-grandchildren.

We sisters have one more moment with you, but you are tiring. So am I. The stress of being here, fearing that I will hurt you, is deepening. We say goodbye.

I hug you once more and tell you I am sorry I have been such a crappy daughter. For years, I disappointed you and Dad. This disease, which took your mental faculties, has mercifully taken that disappointment away from you, but it lives in me. It will live in me forever.

You are asleep before I finish my sentence. Good. *No time for maudlin crap.* For a moment, I can't think at all. I want to pull you back from death, to drag you into life. It seems almost possible – after all, your mind returned to touch the images of your babies. I want to pull you, body and soul, back to life.

The aides show me where to drop my gloves and wash my hands. They tap the codes for the elevator. In the lobby, the lab coat and mask are placed in a plastic bag. I am let out into the rainy afternoon.

Sitting in my car, I feel the tears rolling down my cheeks. I call my daughter, just to talk. Then I pull out of the parking lot, numb and afraid I will never see my mother again.

At 1:50 a.m., my sister calls. You have passed. Without pain. Without protest. The way Dad wanted to go – and wanted you to go, too. None of your babies were there. Lisa has already spoken to the care home, the funeral director, the hospice care nurse. There will be no funeral mass, no wake. A short service, with not more than six people. Six. An impossible number, even in our small family. I can't be in the same room as Lisa, although maybe, in a big funeral parlor room, I can stand at the back door.

Lisa asks if I want to watch you, as they get you ready. I am horrified, but try not to sound that way. It's a fair question, as the cameras were my idea – I bought them, installed them, maintained them. *No,* I don't say, *I don't want to see them put Mom in a body bag.* As I speak other, gentler words, Joe turns off the cameras.

Lisa will call Ginny, who would be angry if we waited. Also, Ginny often looked at the cameras at night, just to see. It's odd. Whenever I checked the cameras, you were happy, thanking an aide or a nurse, laughing, or at worst, asking for help to the bathroom. Ginny only seems to see you angry, yelling, waving your hands at an aide, caught at your worst. Yet we all wanted the cameras to stay.

This morning, there are things to discuss, things to decide.

I must write the obituary.

I can't find the words, so I sift through various cloud drives for pictures. It's hard – you were a modest woman, most of the pictures

I find are you in a group or with Dad. There are, however, treasures:

Pictures of you laughing so hard that your eyes squint shut and you can hardly stand up. I love those.

Pictures of you with babies and toddlers on your lap. Babies and toddlers like it there.

Pictures of you being silly and dignified, all at the same time. Those are terrific, too.

All of a sudden, I can write.

A DREAM IN THE TIME OF CORONA
Susan D. Corbin

Mother has been dead now for eleven days.
I dreamed of her last night.

In the dream, I told her I was sorry
I couldn't hold her hand
While she lay alone and dying during the pandemic.
Even though she didn't have the scourge,
They wouldn't let me in until it was too late and
    she was gone.

In the dream, I told her I'd tried to be a good daughter.
In the three years that
She'd had dementia
And lived in the nursing home
With strangers

Changing her diaper,
Dressing her,
Bathing her,
Doing her hair, and
Giving her meds.

In the dream, I told her that I did what I could.
Visited her and brought the silly dog,
Brushed her hair and did her nails,
Called her on the phone
And talked until she nodded off to sleep.

In the dream, I told her it broke my heart
That when she asked, I couldn't take her home.
I wasn't even sure my home
Was the place she meant,
Perhaps she wanted Illinois or Houston.

In the dream, I told her how much I appreciated
The love she had shown my siblings and me,
As she raised us as an almost single mother
With our slowly withdrawing
And disappearing father.

In the dream, I told her
I love her
Miss her
Think of her
Every day.

PANDEMIC CENTO
Ann Haas

This cento poem was created from headlines and quotes from the NY Times and the local newspaper's articles, obituaries, and from poems by Billy Collins and Ellery Akers.

May 25, 2020

Rise in domestic violence and child abuse
Safety nets sidelined
Lives were lost as warnings went unheeded
Endurance is…whatever must be borne will be borne.
Next patient. Next after next after next – without a "beginning or end."
…we are forced to live in a continuous present.
Six feet apart
Keeping a distance, from everything but nature
The hidden language of masks…Smithsonian
gathering artifacts of a global pandemic for posterity.
The virus killed an officer. She was a casualty of war.
A hospital mourns a doctor…"I want to be like him;"

Delayed grief will pile up on the shores of tomorrow:
Far right grows louder, emboldened by a crisis
The best interests of our customers and employees in mind,
And wouldn't I like to…
Social distancing, without the police
No such thing as a proper home-going ceremony –
This scourge has killed rituals, too;
Wrung out by grief
She spent her last month of college lifting bodies in a morgue.
Handling life after their lock down:
Choosing courage in the face of the unknown
Relishing traffic, coping with loss, avoiding risk
I wish I could do something for you, my doctor said
Doctors and nurses should think more about their necks –
I read about you in the newspaper;
I'm better off closing the newspaper,
…because reading the news was like opening a freezer
and smelling stale ice:

NOT MY HOUSE
Antoinette Carone

I am not living in my own home anymore. Rather, I should say, not my own house. My home is where I make it and now I live with the man I love. His home has become mine.

He has owned this place for many years. Therefore, the things that surround us were here long before I came. That is not to say I don't like them. I do. But they tell stories apart from my own. When we closed our apartment in New York City and went to stay in Long Island, I left most of my history there.

Recently a friend asked me which object in my home gives me the most comfort now that we are all constrained to spend time indoors and keep our distance from friends and family. Most of what I have is now beyond my reach. Yet even though I have never wanted a lot of possessions, I do miss certain ones. Mostly the ones that have memories attached.

Like the candy dish I bought in Venice. My late husband and I went to Italy and we brought our two children with us. I hope the kids have some memories of that trip because I don't think they will be able to travel in these times. But they were very young, so I don't know.

We hadn't planned where we would go in Italy. We simply drove, and ended up just outside Venice. Vehicles were not permitted beyond that point, so we parked the car and checked into a nearby hotel (which proved to be inexpensive and cozy), then went out walking. We crossed a bridge and there we were – in Venice. Canals had replaced roads; boats had replaced cars.

We couldn't afford a ride in a gondola, but the kids were happy with the water taxi that cost only a few thousand *lire*. (About 1500 *lire* equaled one dollar. It was a long time ago.) Afterward we wandered around, just looking at everything.

I bought the kids *Oranginas*. My four-year-old daughter dropped hers in front of the doorway of an elegant glassware boutique. I was mortified. Sticky orange liquid spread across the entrance. No one could have gone in without wading through the puddle. I didn't know what to do.

The owner came out with a pail of water and a broom.

"Don' worry, Signora. It was an accident." He threw water on the mess and swept it away.

In the meantime, the glassware in the window caught my eye. My husband stayed outdoors with the kids while I went inside. There I purchased a small fluted candy dish with pink and green stripes. Nothing like I would have bought for myself before. I wanted to thank the owner for his graciousness, yes. But I really loved that piece of glass.

My kids are far away from me now and I miss them. As for the candy dish, whenever I handled it, I would think of that beautiful, mischievous little girl, who could wreak havoc and bring joy at the same time.

BLUE, RED, AND WHITE
Laura Maurer Goodell, MD

BLUE

Lindsey startled awake in the chair. *I must have drifted off to sleep.*

She ran to check on her three-year-old son Ben, who had had a fever and cough.

Ben's chest was barely moving. His lips and fingers had a bluish tint.

"Ben," she cried as she shook the boy. "Wake up, wake up! Mommy's here."

"Jeff!" she screamed to her husband. "He's barely breathing! We have to go to the ER now!"

The ten-minute drive to the hospital took an eternity.

"Jeff, drive faster, drive faster! Ben, don't leave me! Wake up, wake up!"

But as Jeff parked the car, grabbed the child, and ran through the doors of the ER, Lindsey slowly followed, knowing there was nothing to be done for Ben.

Her son, her baby, was not moving. He was blue and still.

Ben was dead.

RED

The young woman set the grocery bags on the kitchen table.

"Here you are, Grandma and Grandpa. I think I got everything on your list."

"Thank you, Sophie. Did you get a sunburn at the beach?" Grandma asked.

"Maybe a little on my face. And my eyelids are super red. But it's okay."

"What's that rash on your arm?" Grandpa demanded.

"I don't know. My toes are kind of red and swollen too. And my sense of smell seems off. It's kind of strange. But I'm fine."

"You don't have that coronavirus, do you?" asked Grandma, looking worried.

"Oh no, I don't have a fever. I'm not coughing. I don't have coronavirus."

Two weeks later, Grandma and Grandpa were both dead.

WHITE

Christina wore white. White hood, white mask, white suit, white gloves.

"Dr. Jackson," she asserted, "the patient Robert Smith in ER bed #3 is gasping. His oxygen is at 100%. The ventilators are full. What do I do?"

"Do?" asked Dr. Jackson, as he turned away. "There is nothing to do."

Christina grabbed his arm. "But doctor, but doctor, he looks terrified. Help him, please."

"Fine. Just turn up the morphine," he said, as he shrugged and slowly walked away.

She opened the IV drip.

As Christina held Robert's bare hands with her gloved hands, he seemed to calm as he drifted off to sleep.

My angel, were Robert's last thoughts, *my angel has come.*

MENTORING AND COVID-19
Kalí Rourke

I recently received a certificate from Seedling Mentoring, celebrating seven years of mentoring children who deal with having a parent in prison. I have worked with Seedling as a Board Member since its inception fifteen years ago, and for the last few years, I have been active on its Advisory Council and doing weekly mentoring in Austin's public schools.

I am matched with my second mentee now, and we have been together for kindergarten, first, and second grades. We have become good friends who read, play, and laugh together. I don't take that lightly. Children of trauma let you into their lives in various ways and layers of depth and it took me a year to earn a hug from this little one.

She is not shy, but she is reserved until she trusts you. She looks at you with those big brown eyes that seem older than her years and yes, you are being judged. Are you safe? Are you reliable? Are you going to be too shocked by her story to want to be her friend? Are you going to abandon her?

Children who have a parent in prison often live *undercover*. Incarceration can be considered shameful, so if you have a parent who is or has been there, you keep it on the down-low, and only trusted friends are allowed to know. These children have often lost more than a parent. They may have lost their childhood home, the family may have fragmented, and valuable learning time may have been lost in the chaos.

When Seedling created the mentoring program in 2005, along with other game-changing decisions, they made it mandatory that the child knows the truth, that the Mentor knows the truth, and that the child knows that the Mentor knows, and so they are safe to talk with about this sensitive subject: Genius.

Covid-19 hit at spring break for Austin schools this year and threw a spanner into the works of one-to-one mentoring of these children.

We were not able to do the very important work of closure. Closure is a loving process of saying goodbye, sharing how you feel about each other just in case life sends you down different paths, and often it is one of the few healthy goodbyes these kids have ever experienced.

We can send emails to each other through Seedling for the summer, and I do, but everything is very up in the air about this fall. Even if school opens back up in pandemic-safe ways, I fear that personal mentoring will be curtailed. It is just one more contact that the schools can easily avoid, among so many they cannot. And truthfully, if it was possible, I am in a high-risk age and health group and it would be a risk I would not feel comfortable taking.

Friends say, "What about virtual?" Hmm...maybe. But I can tell you from personal experience that the attention of a young child is hard enough to engage and keep in person.

I don't know if I will see my little friend again until after a vaccine is found and the world gets back on its axis – and that makes me sad.

ONE TOO MANY
Debra Dolan

One too many disappointments
One too many promises not kept
One too many sudden bursts of anger unwarranted and misdirected
One too many accusations
One too many deflections of blame
One too many examples of 'passive aggressive' behaviour
One too many apologies never spoken
One too many "I am not wearing a mask"
One too many expressions of love too late and for wrong reasons
One too many blaming language
One too many "I forgot"
One too many interruptions
One too many 'get out of jail' cards used
One too many actions not congruent with words
One too many "I am not discussing"
One too many times left waiting
One too many sexist, homophobic and COVID propaganda remarks
One too many asking for the same thing over-and-over, not accepting
    response

One too many fucks without kissing
One too many "I thought it would be funny"
One too many calorie-laden dinners accompanied by free-pours
One too many treating me like property
One too many abandoning myself

WHAT I MISS ABOUT LIVING WITH COVID:
THE SMILES
Claire Butler

As a single woman who works from home, I initially thought that quarantining would be *business as usual* for me. I am an artist and a writer, both solitary occupations. I am also a smiler—I like giving and receiving smiles.

Before the mandatory quarantine, I started my mornings by sitting on my private little patio, surrounded by trees and flowers, writing in my journal while sipping morning coffee. In the tower of the centuries-old church close by, the bells rang on the hour, and on Sundays they played hymnal songs that I remembered from my childhood. I watched hummingbirds feed, squirrels flip and loop through the trees, and breathed in the fragrance of my small flower bed only a foot away from my outdoor table. On most mornings, only the breeze made sound rustling the adjacent trees. I gave no consideration to what might lay ahead, as I believed that my world would little change as I was used to being alone. But I was wrong.

In April, Ohio's governor declared the entire state would shut down. The quarantine required us to stay home for an indefinite period of time—we could leave our homes only for essential reasons. The bells in the church tower stopped ringing as there was no one to oversee them. My neighbor opened her in-ground pool to children of family and friends to spend down their energy, disturbing the tranquility of my little patio. The ruckus stopped the birds from visiting and the squirrels disappeared. As the months rolled on with no end to the pandemic in sight, sitting on my patio with its flowers and old stone walls was no longer appealing. Journaling was no longer the early morning blessing it once had been. Writing and painting suddenly seemed like work instead of joy, and loneliness crept in. Mandatory quarantine was different from the voluntary one, as I had not realized before just how many times I left the house in a day.

After the state-wide quarantine was lifted, wearing gloves and masks, wiping everything down, including the mail, washing hands and using hand sanitizer at every opportunity became the constant message from the Press and social media. Hoarding made acquiring the simplest of needs a hardship. The cost of food was on the rise, and meat became scarce. Ordering groceries from local stores with drive-up delivery meant I had to order five days ahead due to demand. People were afraid to encounter others and mentally paced off six feet—personal space between themselves and every stranger they met while running errands—something they had never done before.

Of course all of that was a sad state of affairs, but what I missed were the smiles from friends and strangers. One day I counted more than ten encounters without smiles. Tempers seemed to flare more easily. Perhaps the burden of mask wearing was taking its toll, when combined with the record high temperatures we experienced in June and July, causing excessive facial sweating and fog for those wearing glasses. Still, I tried to imagine what their smiles would look like.

A smile is friendlier than a handshake, and it is often the only form of communication between strangers as they pass by one another. It can be both a greeting and a farewell. Its offering can make your day. A smile separates us from other mammals, and living without them for months makes me long for that silent, gentle piece of humanity that once was. Mask wearing is a sacrifice that we make in the name of good public health. We do it for the safety of others and ourselves. I pray that when the pandemic is over, our smiles are not frozen in the past, but rather emerge with an energy not seen in months, because a smile is a gift we give to others. Above all else, that is what I miss.

DISRESPECTFUL OF HIS TIME
Lisa A. Seel

Dad was stalwart. On his own at 89, he still cooked his meals, drove and maintained his car, and managed his finances. He lived in a small senior apartment complex, and took great care of himself. Occasionally he'd go golfing with Al, who lived across the hall; but if not, he'd do squats and lift weights to keep his muscles from atrophying. "Use it or lose it." was his motto. I often joked that he was in better shape than me! I wasn't the only one who noticed...he was always surrounded by a harem of silver-haired divas. When I'd arrive in the lobby, he'd stand and announce, "Sorry ladies, my number one gal is here," leaving them speechless, mouths agape.

Even at 89, Dad's mind was sharp. He sang and played the piano regularly, remembering all of the words from songs he sang in his youth. He attended weekly bible study, and managed to use the smartphone we got him—something that many his age wouldn't even try! Dad was my hero.

On a relatively warm day in December, the noontime sun had reduced the snow to a dirty slush. Dad's immaculate 1997 Buick LeSabre sat in a shaded spot of the parking lot outside his apartment. Even when he had no place to go, he'd go outside and start the car, letting it idle for a few minutes. He was a man of routine.

"Headin' out today, Charlie?" a voice yelled across the parking lot. It was Bob, the building's handyman. He had just come to throw more salt on the sidewalk.

"Nah, just making sure it's runnin' okay. You don't want 'em to sit too long in this weather." Dad patted the bumper showing his affection, and headed to the driver's side of the car.

After a few minutes, Bob noticed that Dad's car never started. Looking up from his work, he saw that Dad was not in sight. Thankfully, Bob investigated. Dad was lying, unresponsive, on a small patch of ice that still remained by the driver's-side door.

———

The events of the next 24 hours are a blur. One minute I was answering a call from the apartment's management about an accident; the next I was sitting in the trauma ER at the hospital, waiting for someone to give me an update. I don't remember much except for donning the mask that the receptionist handed to me. "Flu season is here!" she chirped. "They took him directly to surgery. He was alert but in pain. I'll have someone come out to talk to you as soon as we know more." Finally, after hours of waiting, a doctor in scrubs came to me.

"Your dad is doing well," was, thankfully, how he started the conversation. "He's a strong man and in tremendous shape for his age. We had to put two rods in his back and several screws, but I think…" That was all I heard before sobbing took over. Dad was alive; that was all that mattered.

The next six weeks proved to be tough for Dad; he resolved to be tougher. Constant PT, OT, meds, and evaluations were no match for him.

"Now you know, Mr. Mayfield, you can't go back to your apartment." The social worker's eyes darted to mine before landing on Dad.

"Just temporarily, right? Until I can get around safely?" His hope sprang eternal.

She continued telling him about the ongoing therapy, and the wonderful amenities that assisted living facilities offered. Finally, her voice trailed off as she realized she was not convincing him. "Some are like staying in a 5-star hotel…" His silence continued. Sensing it was best to leave us to think about things for a while, she exited, adding, "I'll be back to check on you tomorrow, Mr. Mayfield."

"This is bullshit." Dad boomed as the door closed. "I have things to do. I was just telling Danny that I'd head upstate to see him and Ellie this summer. Now she wants to put me in a goddamned home. I wanna go see that new grandnephew of mine, too. That kid'll be in college by the time I make it out to Jersey." Dad's voice became increasingly shaky, and a single tear slid down his cheek. "I need more time." He whispered and closed his eyes.

I leaned over and kissed him.

———

The lobby of *Twin Pines Senior Living* looked like that of a luxury hotel. After a wonderful lunch in the dining hall, the leasing manager assured us that Dad would be very happy in his new apartment. Dad was quiet, but polite. His eyes lit up when she showed him the baby grand piano in the lobby and told him that it was there for residents to use. Again, she assured him that he was free to come and go as he pleased, and had full access to all facilities and activities…even the gym. It was almost March, and she talked about the outdoor activities they had planned for nicer weather. I could see Dad's reluctance was slowly waning.

The first three weeks were great. Dad was getting comfortable in his new place and recovering remarkably. I'd visit daily, and he'd talk about his plans for getting out. The Buick was parked just outside his window, and a young aide had agreed to start it every day for him. Things were looking up.

As I left Dad's apartment on a warm Friday in March, the activities director, who had taken a liking to Dad, stopped me in the hallway. "I hear that we will be restricting visitation starting Monday. I guess this Coronavirus thing is going crazy. I'm sure it won't be for long…just until they can sanitize everything and establish some protocols. I just wanted to give you a heads up."

I thanked her and headed home. Only loosely following the outbreak, I heard that the first cases had just hit our area. But, contradicting information and uncertainty kept most people, like myself, from taking it too seriously.

When I told Dad the news on Saturday afternoon, he growled, "Just another waste of time."

"Daddy, I'm sure it'll only be a couple days. Take advantage of it… build your strength so you can get out."

"Hmmph."

As I kissed him goodbye, I reminded him that I wouldn't see him for a few days—a knot twisted in my stomach. "I'll call you tomorrow… promise." He squeezed my hand and I left.

———

"Restricted visitation" turned into a total lockdown at the end of the first week. At the end of week four, Dad was scheduled for a follow-up with the surgeon. Given his remarkable progress, he was sure he'd be allowed to move out of the "prison," as he began to call it.

Unfortunately, he wasn't allowed out for the follow-up. Frustration and anger took over Dad, as sadness and despair gripped me. I would sit in the parking lot below his apartment window and talk to him on the phone, just to see his face.

Spring turned to early summer, and Dad's frustration turned to confusion. Our conversations no longer consisted of happy chatter. Dad was blaming me for his "imprisonment." Our relationship became more strained as time wore on. Still, no one allowed in or out of *Twin Pines*, except staff. It was four months since I'd actually seen Dad.

In the early morning of July 11th, the facility called. "Ms. Mayfield?"

"Yes," tears formed.

"We are taking your Dad to the hospital. He is running a fever and having difficulty breathing. The ambulance is here now. Can you meet us there?"

I threw on clothes and rushed to the hospital, pulling in right behind the ambulance. Pushing past the EMT, I grabbed my dad's hand, "I'm here, Daddy."

In a low, strained voice, Dad managed, "Sweetheart, they've wasted what little time I had."

"I'm sorry, Miss," said the EMT. "Visitors are prohibited because of the virus."

It was the last time I saw Dad. He lasted two more days before they intubated him. After that, it was a few hours. When the nurse's station called to say Dad had passed, all I could muster was "Okay" before hanging up.

COVID-19 had mercilessly taken the last bit of time my dad had on this earth.

HAIKU FOR OUR TIMES
Thelma Zirkelbach

I'm washing my hands.
"Happy Birthday, Happy Birth—"
I need a new song.

Cat's head on my arm,
She looks up at me and purrs.
We aren't lonely.

Play Mah Jongg online,
Can't cough at each other.
Technology's great.

A champagne party—
Drinks and snacks at our
    doorways.
We toast from afar.

We're all in lockdown.
Imprisoned by the virus,
We gaze at empty streets.

A game of Scrabble.
But are we six feet apart?
Who cares? I got Z.

Check the Dow hourly,
Watch my finances dwindle.
Will I need welfare?

My hair's going gray.
Looking in the mirror now
I see my mother.

Is this the first wave
Or is it the second wave?
Whatever…still home.

Connection to the world,
What would we do without Zoom,
Our Covid savior?

Who is that masked man?
Is he a dangerous guy?
Oh, it's my neighbor.

Missed the bluebonnets.
Missed the azaleas.
Spring has passed me by.

Comfort

A Mother's Lessons in Endurance and Resilience
Hendrika de Vries

The age of COVID-19 has pushed the pause button on our twenty-first century fast-track lives. A global virus has cancelled family visits, book tours, school presentations, and social time with friends. The shock of it all sent me into a funk, until I remembered the lessons my mother taught me when she and I sat huddled together in our cold apartment in Amsterdam, hoping to survive another day.

I was seven years old. The freedom-loving city of my birth, Amsterdam, had changed into a city of despair. A virus called hatred, spread by Nazi oppression and brutality, threatened anyone considered weak, "inferior" or disposable. In fear and distrust, people went into hiding to save their lives. In the midst of one of the coldest winters on record, all electricity and gas had been turned off indefinitely. Food supplies were cut off. Grocery store shelves stood empty. Many people, isolated and alone, slowly succumbed to starvation and suicidal hopelessness. So many died, the city of Amsterdam ran out of coffins. School children, bundled up in layers of winter clothes, only attended class a couple of hours a day. Time stood still, as we waited for the Hunger Winter, the name historians would give it one day, to end.

I never dreamt that seventy-five years later I would revisit the tools my mother, a master at endurance and resilience, gave me during those final dark days of WWII, so that I could adjust to life on COVID time.

Our human relationship to time has always fascinated me. It began on my daddy's lap as a little girl when he told me the stories that started with "Once Upon a Time...." Most of my life has been lived in the fast lane that demanded careful planning of time. My life achievements and satisfaction depended on stopwatches, alarms, calendars, and schedules. I was a teenage competitive swimmer, my coach walking alongside the pool recording time with his stopwatch as I swam my laps. The goal was to "break the existing time," whether one's own or that of a competing swimmer. Later, as I went back to school, a single mom of three children, earning my degrees depended on being able to balance time. I went into psychoanalysis, where my analyst marked the end of each analytic hour with: "time is up." I said it to my own clients when I became a therapist myself. My calendar for the year 2020 organized time with schedules for book tours, middle and high school student presentations, week-long visits from adult children, and family birthday celebrations to mark "special times" – 21 years for my granddaughter, 60 for my son. My time was full. I loved it. And then COVID-19 abruptly brought my full and rich, fast-track life to a screeching halt.

As I grieve and shelter at home amidst the escalating fear, distrust, and vulnerability that permeates our nation, I hear my mother's voice, "Wear your mask, wash your hands, keep that social distance." If she were still alive, she would also be reminding me to watch my attitude, express gratitude, practice discipline, and nurture my faith and hope, as she did when I was a little girl.

My mother grew up in a time when death was more present in the family home than today. She lived through the Spanish flu pandemic when she was eight. When her mother would not let her play outside, she sat at the window in a huff and watched endless lines of horse-drawn carts loaded with coffins pass by. She was not afraid of mortality and had great faith in the meaning of things, but she did not believe that life was all about pleasure and bliss. It involved grit and courage. When the Nazis occupied Amsterdam and my father was deported to a prisoner of war camp in Germany, she joined the Resistance and brought a Jewish girl to live with us. Her actions modeled feminine heroism, the courage to stand up to bullies and speak up for those who are being victimized.

Even after she was betrayed and the girl we had sheltered was taken away, when survival seemed beyond hope, she refused to let us think of ourselves as victims.

"We are all heroes and heroines in our own story," she told me in her matter-of-fact voice, "and heroines have to endure trials to make the world a better place."

At a time when freedom from oppression was for many of us merely a fantasy, my mother's fierce spirit showed me an inner freedom that gave me strength and faith.

She insisted on daily prayers of gratitude. "We have a home," she said. "We have each other. We are alive and that means we have hope."

She taught me to focus on the things under my control. Each day I made my bed, brushed my teeth, and washed my face and hands. "We can keep ourselves clean," she said, even though the water was icy cold, and we had long run out of soap, and yes, toilet paper.

I learned that survival depended on discipline and planning, and that delayed gratification could be a gift, not a punishment. If we divided one loaf of bread, the ration for that week, into a slice a day, we could survive. If we ate it all in one day, we might not.

My mother never denied the reality of the danger we were in. She acknowledged grief and fear but used imagination and ritual to ease it. When our daily food supply dwindled to one slice of bread made of tulip bulbs, I had trouble sleeping, because I was scared that there would be nothing to eat when I woke up. She put the slice of bread in a colorful pan next to the bed, where I could see it. If I woke up during the night, as I often did, the sight of the orange pan that held its slice of bread reassured me. I could sleep.

Locked into COVID time, many of us are grieving and feeling scared. How do we acknowledge and honor our collective and individual fears and grief at time lost? My memory of the bright orange pan beside my bed reminds me of the unique ways we each cope with grief and fear. For some of us, the equivalent of the orange pan may be a card in the mail, a phone call or a FaceTime, Skype, or Zoom, perhaps a meal, or garden veggies left at the door. With time being more fluid now, some of us alternate between a desire to nap or tune out and a need to hear stories of courage and resilience.

My mother loved biographies, and her retelling of the life stories she had read or heard filled our lonely days with the palpable presence of historical figures, of ancestors, and family members whose antics, foibles, and achievements my mother admired or found reprehensible. I learned about the lives of real men and women and the hardships that infused their blood and bones with determination and fortitude, a strength, my mother assured me, that lived in me, too.

I always thought of my mother as a heroine, but today I treasure the simple daily skills she taught me to cope with difficult times. In that lonely apartment in Amsterdam long ago, where one day was much like the next, with not even a radio to break the monotony, my mother armed with her biographies, faith, and practical tasks of survival, challenged me to imagine a better world and practice the skills and attitude to act on it. We survived the unspeakable then. Because of her, I can embrace life on COVID time and imagine it as a wellspring for the stories of endurance and resilience that today's children, envisioning a better world, will tell their future children: "Once Upon a Time… there was a pandemic."

THE TEMPTATION OF QUARANTINE
Judy Alter

I remember clearly that last day before we quarantined. It was March 12, and I had a talk to give to the book club group at the Arlington (Texas) Woman's Club. Although I'm told I'm an excellent public speaker, I always work myself into a nervous snit before a talk. This day I was grateful that my friend Subie and her sister, Diana, went with me. They provided transportation and comfort. The talk went well—lots of laughter, which is always a good thing—and I gathered several requests to speak to other groups, none of which will materialize now because of the quarantine. At the lunch that followed there was talk that this was probably the last meeting of the group, because they would go into quarantine. But the idea seemed remote.

That evening my friend Carol and I had supper at Lucille's, an American bistro-style place we both like because it is comfortable, the food good if neither unusual nor outstanding. It's just easy. I don't remember what I ate, but it was probably either their cheeseburger—charbroiled and delicious—or the lobster bites. I do remember we remarked on how empty the restaurant was and wondered if people were already staying home because of the virus, which hadn't yet hit us in any significant numbers.

In the next four months I went out of the house exactly five times: twice to the doctor, once to the dentist (took courage on my part but they followed strict sanitary and isolation measures), once to a neighbor's back yard, and once with my daughter, Jordan, to pick up to-go food.

At first, I think quarantine scared everyone, as though there were no way we could isolate enough to escape this monster that was all around us. Gradually, we began to see what worked and what didn't. We ordered groceries, disinfected the mail, and doused ourselves with hand sanitizer at every turn.

I fell into a routine, spent my days in the clothes I'd slept in and then cleaned up and "dressed" for supper. I never wore make-up, though when I saw myself at a few Zoom meetings, I realized lipstick would probably be a good idea. One of my sons once said I have a fetish about washing my hair daily, but I gave that up, too, and went to every other day, or sometimes (gasp!) every third day. I worked at my desk all morning and napped heavily in the afternoon. My family came to my cottage most nights for supper, so I had some companionship. And the nights I was responsible for dinner, I cooked in the late afternoon. That was a joy, because I like to cook, and I like to feed my family. I never went anywhere, so we had to remember to start my car occasionally lest the battery die. I didn't read as many books as I expected to. There was too much else going on.

After the first panicky weeks, we began to invite one or two people for a distanced happy hour, BYOB, on the patio. We only invited those we knew were also quarantining in the way we were. It was good to see people again and to talk, often of politics.

And suddenly, one day, I realized I was utterly content. It came to me that I could spend my life that way—writing, reading, cooking, and napping. Oh sure, I missed lunches and dinners in restaurants with friends, trips to the grocery. In my few trips out, just seeing what was going on in the neighborhood and beyond amazed me—a house torn down here, a new building there. But I was happy, even relaxed.

All my adult life I have battled an anxiety disorder. Yes, I have had anxiety attacks and panic attacks. There is a blanket diagnosis out there often used for anxiety disorder—agoraphobia—but I prefer not to use it. I don't want to give my monster that much power.

Although fear has long been a part of my life, I wouldn't want you to think I've lived my entire life trembling in terror. I've had a wonderful life—four terrific children and seven grandchildren I adore, a marriage that was mostly happy before it went south, a good career doing work that I enjoyed, and, I hope, maybe helped a few other people, the love of a couple of really good men. I own my home, live comfortably in the cottage behind it while my youngest daughter and her family live in the house. But always, lurking behind the good times, was the fear.

I don't like to drive beyond the limits of my rather confined comfort zone; heights make me dizzily out of control; I don't want to ever swim again—I love looking at water but don't want to be in or on it; the dentist brings back my childhood fear; I can't make myself ride in a self-service elevator alone. And the list goes on. It's like having a basket of small phobias. But with quarantine, I no longer have to gear myself up to drive downtown or give that speech or go to a meeting in a building with a self-service elevator. I can stay in my amazingly comfortable cottage, content, with my dog for company.

Quarantine and the subsequent isolation are easier for me than many because I'm retired and work at home, as a writer. I was pretty much used to staying home most days by myself. In the last few years, I've rarely gone shopping by myself—being on a walker made it difficult and, my daughter said, made me vulnerable. So I'm used to a certain level of isolation and limited activity.

Now some of the changes from quarantine will become permanent, and I have to think long and hard about that. I did not renew my driver's license when it came due and must figure out what to do with my classic VW Bug convertible. Would I give up my nap for a long and late lunch out? Do I really want to go to that lecture or see that exhibit? The downside to all this is that it puts a burden on my daughter and, to a lesser extent, on my friends. Jordan must drive me to doctor appointments, though they are fewer now that my health has stabilized (knock on wood). When we can once again comfortably go to restaurants, church, and a few other places, I will have to rely on family and friends to get me there. A part of me is looking forward to those times, crafting a compromise between quarantine and a limited social life.

Then again, who knows? I may tire of the isolation, especially if the writing well runs dry. But for now, for me, it's not all bad.

WINDOWS TO THE WORLD
Thelma Zirkelbach

Through my bedroom window, sunlight pricks my eyelids and wakes me each morning. Until the virus attacked us, the window was just a pane of glass. Now it's a link to the world, a tenuous one at that, but still a connection.

While the coronavirus rages outside, the residents of our building are sheltering in place. We're healthy, energetic people but we belong to a vulnerable age group, so we're urged to be careful. No visitors, masks whenever we leave our apartments, no close contacts, no large events, no dining room service. Meanwhile, life in the city continues at a slower pace, with less traffic than usual, with shuttered stores and restaurants, hair salons and gyms.

My window affords me views of the world that's inching along without me. If I look down, I see the black-shingled roofs of the apartment house next door. This is not an attractive sight; however, if I lean my forehead against the window and look left, I can see the edge of the nearby bayou and recall two years ago when Hurricane Harvey slammed into Houston. Water rushed over the banks, turned streets into rivers and covered lawns with water that reeked of sewage, forced its way into houses and demolished furniture, drenched books and destroyed treasured mementos, leaving the city a soggy mess.

Farther left are buildings surrounding the Galleria, where I could shop or browse in pre-COVID days that seem so long ago.

If I look straight ahead, I can see the buildings of the Texas Medical Center, the largest medical complex in the world. Hospital beds are becoming scarce these days with virus cases roaring through Texas. To the right I can see NRG stadium where the hapless Texans play football and, predictably, deny Houston's yearly dreams of a Super Bowl appearance.

Upward is the sky, hazy gray, pale blue, or on some days obscured by threatening black clouds that I hope don't portend another hurricane. At dusk I watch the city's lights blink on and imagine lives going on in other buildings. Are people in those places happy, afraid, hopeful? How has the virus changed their lives?

I prefer to look up at night when stars sprinkle the sky and the endless view reminds me how small Earth is, a pale blue dot in a limitless universe beyond which lie other universes that even our strongest telescopes can't see. How small our troubles seem when I gaze skyward.

———

I have another window to the outside world: technology. I love the little windows on Zoom, where a group of friends meets every afternoon at 4:00 to share what's going on in our lives. Not much these days. But it's a joy to see faces we can't see in person. Last week we toasted virtually to better days ahead.

Zoom allows me the pleasure of listening to lectures or concerts. I've hosted a birthday party, visited my children on Mother's Day, taught a course on writing legacy letters for the nearby YMCA, and had a telemedicine appointment in place of my annual check-up. Last year, I'd never heard of Zoom. Today those tiny windows are a connection I otherwise couldn't have.

———

Robin Williams said, "There's a world out there. Open a window and it's there." Tragically, he closed his window too soon, but he left us a mantra to guide us through these difficult times.

LEGACY BLESSINGS:
A HEALING TRIFECTA FOR THESE DIVISIVE TIMES
Ann Haas

A BLESSING TO RESTORE JUSTICE AND EQUALITY
May we find courageous creativity to revisit the injustices, mistakes, and imperfections that are cycling through our society today and which have exposed the longstanding fissures of inequality that are perpetuated by the history lessons we have ignored.

May we find a creative path to restore justice and equality that our nation needs to heal in these divisive times.

ANAM CARA BLESSING FOR OUR COMMUNITIES
May we find beauty and light in the diversity of our communities. And open our hearts and minds to the joys of new friendships and traditions.

May our inner light illuminate a path to understanding, acceptance and healing in these divisive times.

May we discover our individual *anam cara* and extend it to those relationships we seek to nourish. And find common ground and joy in one another.

CENTO BLESSING TO HONOR OUR LOSSES
IN THE TIME OF THE PANDEMIC
With thanks to Kevin Anderson, PhD, "I Feel Like I'm Losing It"

May your tears be holy water that you catch and gently touch to your lips.

May your tear stained fingers cross over your heart and be a tender gesture of blessing yourself in your life.

May your tears become a healing blessing you give yourself to honor the bravery you've shown by releasing your unshed tears that mire your grief.

Your bravery will not be tarnished by tears. Your tears will cleanse your soul and become an act of courageous self-compassion.

THE WORLD WE LIVE IN
Mary Jo West

I've been sequestered for eight long weeks, abiding by the Corona virus guidelines to curtail the spread of this infectious disease. One day turns into another without anything eventful happening. It is starting to get me down.

Taking a walk on a warm sunny day, I decide to make a short stop at my daughter Lisa's house. When I arrive, she tells me she has to leave for a doctor's appointment.

"Mom, why don't you go with me? After I see the doctor, I'll put the top down, and we can take a drive along the coast."

"Sure sounds good to me." We put our masks on and off we go.

After her appointment, we're driving for about forty-five minutes when she asks me to keep an eye out for the Shake Shack. Her friend Susie told her it's been there forever and is famous for their milkshakes.

We're on the outskirts of Corona Del Mar, when we see an old, dilapidated, brown wooden building with a big sign, "Shake Shack." Making a sharp turn into the parking lot, we're surprised to see the parking lot is full. It's one car in, and one car out, but after waiting twenty minutes, we're able to get a space.

The line to order food and shakes snakes around the building, past the parking lot, and onto a narrow ledge overlooking the ocean. Everyone is wearing masks and trying to maintain the six-feet rule for distancing, but as we get closer to the order window, the line tightens.

While we're waiting, I walk over to a board on the wall at the entrance and see a list of at least two-dozen varieties of milk shakes. Boy, we're in for a treat, I'm thinking. For another twenty minutes, we're both thinking about how good those milkshakes are going to taste. Finally, we reach the window to order.

"Hi," Lisa says to a tall, shaggy, blond young man taking orders. "We'd like two large shakes, one chocolate fudge, and one fresh blackberry, both with whipped cream on top."

"Sorry," he says, pointing to a large red sign in capital letters above the window. "We're out of ice cream."

"Are you kidding? We drove all the way from San Clemente for one of your shakes." She looks up at the sign. "Oh, okay. Mom would you like a café latté?"

"Yes, that's fine."

"Nope, don't have coffee either," he says in a monotone voice.

Lisa thinks for a moment, scanning the menu. Not wanting to hold up the line, she blurts out, "I'll have a Diet Coke and an order of fries. Want anything else Mom?"

I wave my hand, "No, nothing thanks."

All the way home, we eat French fries dipped in catsup, and I enjoy the sea breeze, the beauty of the coastline, and our lively conversation.

By the time she drops me off to my house, I'm feeling relaxed and rejuvenated.

"Thanks, Lisa, I feel so much better. That's exactly what I needed."

LEARNING TO BAKE CHALLAH
DURING A PANDEMIC
Jeanne Zeeb-Schecter

When I turned seventy-six years old this last June, I retired from my homeopathic practice and decided I would devote more time to writing, finish that half-written book, and learn to make braided challah (egg bread) for our Sabbath meals on Friday nights.

Each week, Sabbath ushers in a twenty-four-hour retreat from the pandemic, protests, politics, and the news of multiple wildfires raging across our state. It's a spiritual restart button that allows me to deal with the rest of the week. I wanted to make it even more special by filling our home with the aroma of my own challah.

In her memoir, *Braided: A Journey of a Thousand Challahs*, Beth Ricanti wrote that the practice of making challah brought her back to a peacefulness infused with spirituality. I joined her challah-baking zoom class one Friday two months ago. Beth made it look easy. Impatient to start that week, I launched a search for her favorite, hard-to-find flour. I drove out to Bristol Farms, a half hour away to buy it. I was ready.

By the way, did you know there was a flour and yeast shortage? In my self-absorption due to five months of "staying home to stay safe," it never dawned on me that thousands of women out there were making bread to fill their hours while sequestered at home, many with small children that just want to go back to school and play outside, or cranky teens who are desperate to go back to their social lives. I'm told that punching the air out of a risen ball of elastic dough can be quite cathartic for an overwhelmed mom.

My first attempt at baking bread was comical. I couldn't get the dough to stretch out into strands to braid them. I improvised and made "challah rolls." With my lower lip protruding in a pout, and the slightest dampness in my eyes, I besieged my poor husband with, "I have an advanced degree, I'm a mother, I have grandchildren and great-grandchildren with whom I have spent hours rolling out Play-Doh into coiled snakes, and I can't make three strands of dough long enough to braid." Sniff, sniff. He assured me that the roll tasted great and he had even eaten a second one. I retorted, "But it's not braided!"

During the following two weeks, I talked to Julie, my sister who has been baking bread for most of her adult life. Julie said, "You need to incorporate some bread flour into the recipe to give the dough more elasticity; it has more gluten, which changes how it feels and stretches." No one had bread flour, not even the specialty markets. I went online to buy it from King Arthur's flour site.

They were out of it! Amazon was out of it! Who were all these baking goddesses out there who knew about bread flour? Again, my sister came to my rescue. "Of course, I always have a couple of five-pound bags of bread flour in the freezer. Freezing kills any bugs and keeps the oils in the wheat from getting rancid." How did she and others know these things? Was it a secret cult? My wonderful husband who wanted to keep me from getting crazier than I had already become, drove the hour out to my sister's and brought home bread flour. Now, he's a keeper. Of course, after thirty-four years together, I know that times ten.

Meanwhile, during the week I asked Julie how she learned to make bread. Our mother had made wonderful cookies and cakes, but never a loaf of bread. Julie told me this precious story about the wife of one of her older college professors. He invited my young sister and her new husband to dinner, where Julie met and fell in love with his sprightly, eighty-year-old wife, Mrs. Haussler. She was invited back many times to visit with this woman, who was usually cooking or baking while they talked. "Oh, I talk to the dough," she told Julie. "I give my yeast mixture an encouraging talk...I can tell when the dough hasn't had enough time to properly rise. I just give it a little pat and tell it to take all the time it needs, I'll come back later. And I always say a little prayer of thanks as I put the loaves into the oven. You know, that helps."

This I could understand, since a lot of my work had been based on my feelings and intuition. Maybe this breadmaking was less mechanical than I had previously thought.

I returned to the kitchen that next Friday morning with a more gentle, loving attitude. I set up the yeast two hours before I planned to begin. As I sprinkled the yeast over the sweetened warm water, I said, "Look what I have for you to eat. It's going to help you grow." Then I covered the measuring cup with cling wrap, and wrapped a dish towel around the outside to hold in the warmth. "I know you can do this," I said. Two hours later, the yeast had bubbled up not the inch it had the week before, but a full four inches to the top.

I substituted half the all-purpose flour with bread flour, mixed in the yeast, water, salt and eggs and covered the mixed dough with a damp, warm towel. I set it next to a closed, sunny window away from fans. This time the dough rose much higher in the large mixing bowl. When I lifted the towel a couple of hours later, I smiled, "Look what you did." I rolled it out onto a floured board and kneaded it for several minutes to push out all the air. Then I pinched off a one-inch ball, held it up and said the Hebrew blessing, the same one said in the temple in Jerusalem when bread was sacrificed some 2,000 years ago. I wrapped it in foil to go into the oven to be burned as an offering. Many Jewish women around the world still do this every Friday.

L'dor, v'dor – from generation to generation.

My stretchy dough strands rolled into the perfect length, and I braided them as easily as I had my daughter's beautiful long hair all those many years ago. I covered the two loaves with a towel and let them rest and rise again. We make two loaves to remind us that when the Jews left Egypt and traveled in the desert for forty years before entering Canaan, God left a double amount of manna, a bread-like sustenance, on Fridays, so the women could gather enough for two days and rest on the Sabbath as commanded.

After brushing an egg-and-water wash on the risen loaves and gently pressing in the toppings of dried garlic, onion, poppy seeds and sesame seeds (Trader Joe's "Everything But The Bagel"), I slid them into the preheated oven.

Twenty-five minutes later, as I removed the baked loaves, the house was filled with the welcoming aroma of our approaching Sabbath. "You're beautiful!" I whispered in awe.

Thank you, Beth Ricanti and the late Mrs. Haussler, and thank you, Julie.

UNCERTAINTY
Ariela Zucker

Uncertainty is my mother, in 1938
only fourteen, when she packs her life
in a small bag that should last her
for seven years, as the safety of home
becomes a fading possibility.

Uncertainty is my aunt, only
sixteen years old, when she
leaves her parents to board
a boat to the yearned for
land of milk and honey.

And I as a young mother, forced to
face another war, barraged by
rumors and threats of unconventional

weapons, of mass distraction.
How are we going to protect the children?

Only the old and sickly, they say now.
And although I am the old, the one being placed
in the front line, it is a certain relief.
Only me. Thank you, God, for once
taking care of the kids.

OPPORTUNITIES LOST AND FOUND
Eileen Harrison Sanchez

Lost: A river cruise, book events, hosting Easter dinner, a Broadway show, JULIET lunches, Thursdays with grandchildren, a wedding, and sadly, friends. I could go on but, with the exception of friends, these losses reveal my privilege.

I am a writer, a published author with a debut novel. A debut at 72? Yes, I call myself a perennial, a person with a no-age mindset. Yet, I resisted the call to keep a diary, to document this time. I feared writing would give it life. Give it more importance than deserved. Make it REAL. And how long could this go on anyway? Now I wonder if it will ever end.

In February, my newly retired husband and I spent a weekend celebrating two birthdays of our youngest grandchildren who live in Philadelphia. After our 10-year-old grandson's basketball team collected the 1ˢᵗ place trophies for the season, his 7-year-old sister and I walked to the Pearlman Building to see the costume exhibition. Her poses in front of her choices for "best of the collection" are now favorites in my iPhone Photos. Then my mini tour guide confidently led me across the four lanes of the Ben Franklin Parkway to the new street-level entrance of the grand Art Museum. We both wanted to view our favorite paintings and she wanted to see the Japanese Tea House. When will we be able to continue this newly found shared interest as grandmother and granddaughter?

After that heartwarming weekend, my husband and I took our first snowbird flight to Siesta Key, Florida, to visit family for a week. My "baby brother" and his wife leave New Jersey for eight weeks each year and wanted to share that concept with us "older" Baby Boomers. Yoga on the beach, long leisurely walks to local restaurants, time to finish two books, and no snow – sounds good. Why not? Yet, it isn't meant to be. Not yet. It will remain one of the endless options we were checking off from our Bucket Lists. The international impact of the virus crept in from social media and news report headlines. The four of us decided to cancel our European river cruise planned for September. On our last evening in Florida, at the daily sunset cocktail hour on a palatial patio overlooking the span of beach slipping into the sea, we met a man who had just returned from Milan. We shook hands – of course we did. I worried about that for weeks. Was he the last person I will ever greet that way?

In March, a dear friend was gardening with her husband. They were in the midst of expanding their annual garden with raised beds, enjoying their extra time with his recent retirement. Sadly, we lost him to a massive heart attack. With the loving support of her sons, who drove from Colorado, she was able to begin her life without him. The reality of not being able to comfort her in person, to be present at his funeral Mass, brought home the challenge of the many families that have lost their loved ones to Covid. More recently there have been other deaths within our circles of family and friends. None of the deaths were due to Covid but the virus changed how we can comfort each other, mourn and grieve these people.

My godson was to be married in June. As April numbers for cases of the virus rose, celebrating his wedding as planned was in jeopardy. After much discussion, it was postponed to October. Fall seemed safe and far enough away that life would return to normal. That didn't materialize and recently the venue was restricted from holding indoor dining at least until November. The wedding will happen, although exactly how is yet to be determined. The reception will wait, maybe until their first anniversary. The virus changed how we can celebrate, congratulate, and participate in their joy.

In January, I traveled to Jefferson, Texas, as an official book club selection at the Pulpwood Queens Girlfriends Weekend. In February, I was an invited speaker at a Louisiana college where two professors chose my book as a required text. Several local New Jersey events were held as scheduled but by March 13th all my book events were postponed or cancelled. Discouraged for myself and some author friends that were launching books in Spring 2020, I turned my energy to technology and, of course, Zoom. Virtual events have allowed me to meet and interact with readers and authors in different time zones from the comfort of my home. My writing community has expanded and is richer due to the supportive communal efforts of my publisher, independent bookstores, and numerous online author and reader groups.

I'm retired from a forty-year career in education. For some years, I've controlled the hours that previously were devoted to my workdays. I often say, "I'm so busy I don't know how I had time to work." These days, ex-colleagues don't interfere with my daily agenda, but I have a new colleague: "my twenty-four/seven husband." He's in the process of determining how he will spend his time. We're adjusting. He's still the best thing that ever happened to me. But he's a restless, newly minted retiree and always ready with a project.

My favorite spot to write was in a cushioned wicker chair in a guest bedroom. I outgrew that and took over the dining room. I finally succumbed to my husband's suggestion to move back to the bedroom. With no sleepovers for the immediate future, I created a combo office and guest room.

We got the dining room table back in time for our anniversary. The table was set with our fine china, crystal and sterling place settings. We had a lovely dinner at home. The formal table remains set for the two of us and we use it on evenings we might have gone to a restaurant. For some time, I've resisted cleaning out and reorganizing the closets, attics, and the garage. We did it together. He was right. He loves it when I say that. Our daughters will be grateful someday.

We have three daughters, three sons-in-law, three granddaughters and three grandsons. Three to the fourth power. One of our sons-in-law is a White police detective and another is a Black businessman. The impact of the virus on our daily lives has shifted to the worry of the polarization of demonstrations for Black Lives Matter and Defund the Police. This is a topic that is fraught with emotion for me. I love both these young men. They care for and respect each other. Their wives are sisters. Their children are the future of this country. Have we taught them well? What are they learning?

There are highs and lows. Some have described being on the Coronacoaster. Back in March I ordered t-shirts that declared

QUARANTINI above the image of an oversized martini glass with olives for the classic drink. It was fun to wear them. Dressed in our masks and shirts we got some laughs as we shopped in the local "essential" liquor store. Our lovely backyard gazebo has served as the spot to sip the classic drink. I still wear the shirt but it's not as funny now.

Sunday afternoon drives have substituted for getaway weekends to Philadelphia, the Jersey Shore, our friends' lake house, and city trips to fulfill my husband's wish to visit every major league ballpark. Walking around our neighborhood and bike riding have replaced our gym membership for exercise. Our wedding anniversary gift to each other was a hitch and a bike carrier for our SUV and a list of destinations from our "Rails to Trails" app.

During this time of quarantine, I have reconsidered my wish to downsize to a city apartment. We will stay in this house with too much stuff in the hideaway storage spots and rooms that need redecorating. We can walk to church, to the post office, food stores and my screened gazebo.

Found: Time – endless days that remind me of the summers of my youth, an herb patio garden, flourishing hanging baskets, a backyard that serves numerous birds, small animals, and as a haven for a doe to give birth to three fawns behind the overgrown rhododendron. I found new communication skills, virtual book events, Zoom, a renewed appreciation of our home, and the man I married.

GROUNDED
Letty Watt

"Whatever were you two thinking, walking home barefoot in this summer heat?" My father screamed at us that July day, when my cousin Fred, aged 13, and I, aged 14, decided to walk home from the Golf and Country Club. With my mother's permission, we began the two-mile walk. However, Fred had money in his pocket and he wanted to buy fireworks. So instead of turning toward home on the boulevard, we traveled south towards the highway where there were firework stands. Time and distance meant nothing to us, as we walked then hobbled on and off the hot gravel-covered asphalt and the cool grasses of the bar ditches, until my father pulled up beside us.

"Dad, we were walking to the fireworks stand, so Fred could buy some firecrackers," I replied sincerely.

"Get in this car now," he scolded.

Once home, we were force-marched to our rooms and grounded. Grounded. I can laugh now, but I frequently told my children that I probably would have been in more trouble as a curious kid, if I hadn't been grounded every summer of my teenage years.

Decades passed and I don't believe my feet ever stayed in one place long. A college education that took seven years, one marriage and divorce, and one child to raise as a single parent and teacher. Ten years later, a new marriage and a combined family of three pre-teens, now through college and on with their own lives. Several moves with my husband, job changes, challenges, deaths of loved ones, and hours of golf with friends. My feet stayed busy during those years of working and into retirement. I moved constantly – walking, laughing, telling stories in my head, greeting strangers with a smile.

This March, while I was playing golf with friends in La Quinta, California, the Corona virus exploded nationwide. On the day of our departure, we drove to Palm Springs, looking near the airport for our annual farewell breakfast. The initial shock, that a silent monster was looming over our casual lives, struck us when we found the strip in Palm Springs was empty, store fronts and restaurants closed. No one standing near the Sonny Bono statue. The three of us fell into silence.

At last we found one place still serving food, and it stood nearly empty. The 1950s throwback diner – with stark white painted walls, red vinyl booths, and round red vinyl stools at a soda counter – felt sterile. How fitting.

Standing at the Palm Springs airport was eerie; as we stood away from each other, only a few had masks. Normally, I might stand by the Mountain Goat statue, painted in desert colors, asking a stranger to take my picture with the palm trees and the Goat. Normally, I might buy a souvenir for a friend. Normally, I would strike up a conversation with stranger.

That day was not normal. My friend from Wisconsin and I stood by each other, staring at strangers around us, asking silently in our heads, "Should I be afraid of you? Are you sick? Will I get sick by making eye contact with you?"

For the first time in my life, my head automatically dropped toward the ground when someone walked too close to me. My feet felt heavy; I walked with caution. Landing in Oklahoma didn't change the cautious fear I felt and saw all around me. I had lost my footing in the world. I no longer felt grounded.

When the panic subsided from the initial outbreak of the virus, I looked around the house for projects to begin, projects to complete, stories to write, and rooms to rearrange. I hungered for a normal day. In our yard alongside my husband, we searched for weeds to pull, bulbs to grow, tasks to keep us busy, like a normal day. We silently sat in corner chairs at the back of our yard, in sweatshirts and long pants. He read. My mind wandered, and I began searching my soul, my heart, for comfort, balance, safety, a normal day. No words, no stories, no colorful thoughts came to mind. This was the worst kind of grounded, and out of my control. Two weeks turned into four weeks, then six.

One morning I put on my walking shoes and my spring all-weather coat, and walked out the door with the dog. We plodded up Hidden Hill, then down Hidden Hill, stopping to sniff every mailbox. I walked Lucy-dog home and turned around to walk again. Ten thousand steps, I could do it. I walked up Hidden Hill and turned a new direction, around cul-de-sacs that I hadn't traveled, until coming to another hilltop that overlooked the ancient riverbed. My breathing relaxed and I noticed spring in the trees, in the bushes, the flowers; a few daffodils and tulips remained, while irises of white, peach, pink, and purple bloomed profusely. My feet nearly ran down the hill when I spied a magnolia tree in bloom. At last I felt normal, nature looked normal – but something was different.

The more I walked the better I felt and the more people I began to see out walking their dogs or each other. Having previously read "Living the Fitbit Life" by David Sedaris, I began searching for characters like a Sedaris sighting. I was not obsessive and found no need to walk more than ten to fifteen thousand steps, whereas Sedaris could wear out a Fitbit in two months, racing to reach his goal of 40,000, 50,000 then 60,000 steps. As he stated, "I have been Fitbit-ten." Not me. My Fitbit kept my steps, but I kept my head and opened my eyes to the new normal. A sense of feeling refreshed flowed into my soul.

Our neighborhood had changed, from appearing void of faces and bodies with people at work and children in school, to streets filled with children on bikes, skateboards, parents walking alongside or behind; to retirees walking dogs of every size and bark. Suddenly, one-on-one basketball games appeared like magic in driveways, with moms and dads out of shape and trying their best to outdo the kids. Laughter, tiny voices screaming in delight, dogs barking, birds chirping, fresh air in our lungs, we were new people living in a new world.

One morning I realized what had changed, and so much for the better. Our air smelled fresher, the birds' chirps could be heard throughout the neighborhood and parks, NO traffic sounds blocked the beauty of nature's music. The faces and voices of our neighbors became familiar, along with names. Some people I saw every day, others not so often, but each time I saw someone I began to feel connected. We all shared a common thread.

My husband and I met little Henry and his mother. Henry's eyes gave him a perfect view of our knees. Henry found sticks to play with when he walked. His mother slowly ambled at Henry's two-year-old pace. We stopped and talked often, from a distance. — The man, a birder in his younger days, hobbled his crippled body to the bench at the park on warm sunny days. His binoculars gave him a picture of the world he used to know. We regularly asked about neighborhood birds. His deep and garbled voice shared stories of migrations and his depth of knowledge. — The two sisters, whose sizes filled one bench, once explained that they drove up the hill, as they pointed toward our hidden hill, then sat on the closest park bench to see people. We often waved and said hello; they smiled in return, always willing to talk about the weather.

Time passed, and I thought to myself one day that perhaps being grounded wasn't so bad at this age in life. Being grounded has taken on a whole new meaning, and still my feet keep me going.

EARLY DAYS
Sarah Fine

I'm not sure what all
this fuss is about
everything
looks the same
from the rooftops
I see fewer humans
but the brick wall still
provides many rough
spots where I can
scrabble with my claws
moving watchfully
from window ledge
to the top of the porch
sideways to the next
window and finally
down to a front lawn
less traffic on the street today
I can safely cross
winter's almost over
so foraging for food
has become
a more rewarding endeavor
and there's always
a backyard bird feeder
if I hang by my hind legs
from that most convenient branch
I can shake up the seeds
cause spillage
that's easy to reach
eat at my leisure
I'm not sure
what all this fuss is about

KEEPING PERSPECTIVE IN THIS TIME OF COVID-19
Tracie Nichols

these things come and go
she said, pausing as a pair of
frantic gray squirrels raced over her
pale yellow green gray bark.

when you've lived your first
hundred years you begin to understand
that warning the neighbors and feeding
them sunlight and sugar if

things get dire is really the only
way to go on with things. it really comes down
to whether you love enough to love
through distance and dying and fear

and all that comes with a living
breathing life lived among living
breathing lives inhaling and exhaling
to the same solar rhythm.

Keeping perspective in this time of Covid-19.

PANDEMIC SPRING
Betty McCreary

The promise of the coming spring helps me slog through the depression
I get during the cold, dark months of winter. I look forward to getting
out to the nearby state park to enjoy the fields of wildflowers and look
for returning birds. But this spring is different. Nature has sent us a
deadly virus. We are under city and county orders to stay at home
unless we have to go out to exercise or get groceries. I am sixty-six and
that puts me in the high risk of dying category, if I get the virus.

The local parks close and I retreat to my beach. This is a comfy
lounge chair in my bedroom and the only beach I am likely to visit
this year. I play solitaire and watch TV, keeping up with the news of
the world. I watch videos of an African-American man dying while a

white policeman kneels on his neck. I watch the deaths of others like him. I watch the daily White House Virus Task Force briefings. I often glance away from the puffed up, orange-haired human on the screen and check on the scene outside my window. I distract myself from the insanity with the natural, calming beauty of my backyard. I can see red admiral butterflies and monarchs sipping nectar from the pink and yellow lantana blossoms. There is also a hummingbird feeder with a lovely black-chinned hummingbird in attendance.

The butterflies calm me and the hummingbirds distract me, but the creatures that bring me the most pleasure are the little green lizards, who are in abundance this year. Almost anytime I turn away from the puffed up man on the screen, I look out and spot these guys puffing up their bright pink throat pouches. They move along the tree branches or fence top, and stop. They puff out the pink pouch a time or two and then move on. Then they stop and do it again. This behavior in these male Anole lizards is to attract a female. My grandmother used to say they were "showing their money."

Just like the ubiquitous facemasks and empty store shelves, these little lizards seem to be everywhere. I see them on walks in the neighborhood. One hangs out near the front porch and I have seen at least three different ones at the same time in the back yard. Or maybe there were always that many of them around. It is just that now I have more time sitting at home enjoying nature from my window, making lemonade out of pandemic lemons.

NATURE'S WAY
Jane Gragg Lewis

If...
There were no wars,
      no tsunamis, volcanic eruptions,
            tornados, earthquakes, hurricanes...

No cancer,
    heart disease,
        bacteria, viruses,
           pandemics...

Would there be room for all of us?

NO QUARANTINE FOR SEA CREATURES
Marilea C. Rabasa

"Hello, Bob. And Bob. And Bob. And Bob. And Bob." Gene named them all 'Bob'—easier that way.

Even before quarantine, Gene was a little nutty about this group of eight or nine giant starfish living under seal rock. That's the rock we paddled past a few years ago with a fat seal sunning itself and sitting right on top. Got a nice picture, too, as we paddled on by.

Gene tries to walk on the beach every day during low tide. Winter or spring. Rain or shine. It's about a mile to seal rock, and that's where he found these giant sea stars, clinging to their home at the base of the rock. They can live without water for many hours while they wait for the tide to come in.

What a life for these starfish. Clinging to their rock. Do they ever venture off of it? Do they ever swim around like sea anemones or jellyfish? Or do they stay on their rock in their isolation, avoiding the company of other sea creatures?

Oh Covid! You've turned us into a couple of hermits, Gene and me. We venture out to the store when we have to. And a couple of people even came over recently, six feet apart, no hugs.

"This is surreal, Gene," I whine after they leave. "I miss hugging people. And I miss a closer connection with my grandchildren. I feel like I'm losing time with them."

Bob and Bob and Bob and Bob and Bob don't care about the coronavirus. Or isolation. Or losing time with anyone.

What a simple life they enjoy. It's only humans that make it complicated.

SEEDLINGS
Joan Stevenson

The garden has always been my husband's passion. My role in the garden has been as cheerleader and voyeur. I could watch it grow without getting my hands dirty! This year is different. It is the year Covid-19 consumed my predictable everyday life. As two weeks dragged into three and on to a month, I felt a personal need motivated by the sequester to move on. As everything around me shut down, I needed to grow something! I decided to explore the backyard shed, which was crammed with garden tools, disturbing the spiders and other crawling life forms in search of an incubator. Once found, to my delight there was a packet of Burpee tomato seeds, hybrid beef steak variety, tucked in the tray.

The information on the envelope bragged that it was "the biggest tomato ever," tipping the scale at three pounds and providing a harvest in 75-80 days. I salivated at the very idea of it. I did note that the use by date was 2015, but I felt that fate had revealed these seeds to me and I must soldier forth.

The incubator resembles an egg carton and I decided the window in my sunny bedroom was the perfect spot to usher in the new life. I filled the cubicles with a mixture of potting soil and fertilizer. When I opened the packet, my heart sank. The seeds were so tiny and there were so many of them that I had to be incredibly careful to place only one in each of the twenty containers. Even watering them took care.

Now the waiting began. I was curious and hopeful, watering each day and talking to them. Once many years ago I was substitute teaching in a first-grade class of forty children. I was new and nervous. The project I was overseeing involved forty Dixie cups filled with soil and one bean seed. One at a time, my students tended their seedlings, watering, checking the soil, and noting by drawing a picture of the progress. It took the entire morning to complete that part of the lesson! I felt like I was back in that classroom.

A week passed, and then one morning I noted a break in the soil as the first seedling woke up. Days later, they were in full birth mode as spindly legs wearing leafy top hats reached upward to seek the sun. There were twenty-two in all. Each tiny seed had contained a bundle of nutrients that was all they needed to fuel their growth.

My morning ritual began as the sun peaked over the crest of Mt. Diablo. Like a hovering mother, I searched for any overnight changes. Then one June morning, I decided the time had arrived for them to be moved to more permanent quarters. All but one of the seeds had survived well, but a bird had nibbled at one sprout leaving only a single leaf—it was clear this plant was not giving way. I named it Junior and committed to its special care. We saved ten of the plants and gave away the rest to neighbors and family.

For their new homes, I needed large black plastic tubs. I returned to the garden shed, where I found ten tubs. I was able to arrange them along the side of the back lawn. Filling them with soil and fertilizer and planting was a task that required an assistant.

I answered an ad on NextDoor placed by Tommy, who promised diligent, timely, conscientious work at a reasonable price. At fourteen years old, he was a man on a mission. His goal was a laptop that he had his eye on. Tommy sized up the task, contributed some ideas of his own, and went to work. He was the perfect man to lead my seedlings through a rite of passage to their grownup home.

After each tub was filled with potting soil, Tommy dug a well in the prepared pot and placed three nails in the bottom to provide the iron tomatoes need for healthy green leaves. With a small ceremony, the plants were set in their homes. Tommy shared my empathy for Junior, found her a smaller container, and planted her with special care himself. Dusk was falling as we compensated Tommy for a job well done.

Hanging from the limbs of my plum and apricot trees are fairy lights, synthetic reminders of the fireflies of my childhood summers. I delight in the way their twinkle illuminates the darkness. I consider them the night watchmen of my tomato garden. There is just a hint of glow left when I take over my watch at sunrise to begin the watering routine. For the past thirty years, Bob used an elaborate system of soaker hoses, but as time went on the hoses and connections began to fail. Several times our first clue to a leak was a water bill that left us breathless. Watering is now done by hand.

Standing with a hose in my hand to water eleven thirsty tomato plants left me time to think creatively. A Christmas gift from my mother-in-law many years ago brought thirty roses to our garden. Why not include some vegetables planted among those roses? There were no rules in this garden, so off to the nursery I went. I purchased several varieties of squash…yes, even zucchini…and a spectacular Italian cucumber that I put on a six-foot-high trellis. Adding the vegetables necessitated poring over garden books to understand why some flourished while others did not. My cucumber had large deep rich green leaves but not a single cucumber until I was reminded there was a male and female flower and no cucumber will arrive without a little hanky-panky between them. Instructions on how we humans can facilitate the process were included in my basic gardening book. Using a very finely bristled paint brush, I can pollinate the female flower with the male. Invitro in the garden. Voila! The Italian cucumber has fascinated me with its tendril, an appendage looking like a slender ringlet of hair that stretches out and twines around any suitable support it can find by touch. The stems look like macramé...a fifties crafty plant! The plant's flower morphs into a caterpillar shape that grows and grows, nine to fifteen inches.

Our garden will never make the pages of *Sunset* magazine. Planned and perfectly executed it is not. Eclectic would be a better description. My husband began taking slips from hydrangeas and successfully propagating them. My daughter-in-law is a floral designer and has access to plants that were beyond their marketing peak. She brings them to Bob, who created an infirmary for ailing, homely, and dying plants. They arrive begging for water, wilted around the edges and sad. They are trimmed, fed, and encouraged. Not all prosper but most seem grateful for a caring home. "Bring me your homeless, tempest tossed..." When a plant is ready to thrive, it joins others on the hill. My chemist husband makes jam from the fruit trees, with labels that read, "Hydrangea Hill" jam.

June had arrived and the tiny green tomatoes on my plants grew bigger, but did not ripen. I was growing impatient. Every morning I gave them the pep talk, "You can do this. This is your role, your destiny!" Then one day my husband came into the kitchen and nestled in his hand was our first real beef steak tomato. It weighed just short of two pounds!

I never imagined that a garden could become such a major part of my life. This was always my husband's territory, a large space at the bottom of the hill in our back yard. As we have grown older, the access down a flight of steep, slippery, mossy steps has become treacherous. When I saw how dispirited Bob was at the possibility of giving up his beloved garden, I decided there had to be a way to make it work. The vegetable garden in our back yard has been the perfect answer.

Now when I begin my morning, a one-sided conversation with roses, tomatoes, squash, and cucumbers, I tell them how grateful I am that they have welcomed me into their world. As the reality of the sequester has unfolded, the seeds I planted have given me a tomorrow. The garden has filled me anticipation and hope.

I Saw Glorious
Madeline Sharples

Sometimes even the worst of times
gets a break. Today I certainly did.
I took an early morning walk
and by the time I got
to the beach I saw glorious!
A double rainbow arched over
my Manhattan Beach pier
highlighted by a bright
ray of sun that could have been
the pot of gold at the rainbows' end.
Some say rainbows bring us hope
and signify that everything
will be okay. If those beliefs
are true, today I got a double dose.
I can live the rest of the day
holed up inside in quarantine
without any complaints.

DOING IT ANYWAY
Tracie Nichols

I almost didn't write this

I'm hungry and
I haven't yet eaten today and
My family are crunching on bagels and

I almost didn't write this

But the blue is so clear and
The leaves are so green and
The furled purple buds promise and

I almost didn't write this

Even though words called and
So many are scared and sick and
My words are what I have to give and

I almost didn't write this

Doing it anyway....

Wrongs

STAINED GLASS
Carol Toole

Distraction dulls and deletes the fine details from view until a pandemic's beam penetrates society's stained glass. The pandemic puts all on pause while responders gear up: our leaders mask truth for their own agenda, police stay 6-feet-distanced from communities they serve, hospitals collect those tipped from the margins of society, told to shelter in places already precarious. We are all isolated from ourselves. Warp speed toward a vaccine against returning to normal; protect us from forgetting the fevered voices crying out, lives at risk on our streets: "Now is the time, 400 years late, enough, enough. We can't breathe." Now that we've seen.

TEEN USA
Christine Ristaino

I read that teens were having Coronavirus parties with the sheer goal of catching it from previously diagnosed invitees. The first one diagnosed after the party wins a pot of money. So does it take more than a thousand deaths a day to make one wonder if this is a good idea? How many parents and grandparents will die as a result of this game they don't even know their kids are playing? And what will these children do when the finality of their actions hits them? Fourteen days of a high fever and chills? A sibling in the hospital with complications? A parent on life-support? Somebody dead? When consequences and impulsivity battle, teen USA has been choosing the latter. I find myself secretly calculating when our country will leave its teenage years behind. When I walk the streets of Italy, I feel its ancient history in the names of the streets, in the old, heavy, cracked marble stairs, in the churches that rise from the hills. Italy's Coronavirus numbers are down and people are staying home. But here, everything is still so young and the underdeveloped brain of our country continues to try death-defying feats. Oh, to reach our mid-twenties when finally we love our parents again, start thinking beyond the pot of money, and no longer believe we're immortal.

COVID-19 IS NOT THE ONLY ILLNESS
Teresa Lynn

I stand six feet outside the entrance of the ER, in the middle of the patient drop-off drive, leaning against my husband. One hand clutches my ID, insurance card, and emesis bag; the other presses my stomach. A sullen, tattooed nurse stands in the doorway and asks Covid-19 screening questions: have I developed a recent cough or fever? have I traveled out of the country? have I...?

Each "No," which must project past my facemask, pulls every drop of energy from my core. Most people don't realize words begin in the gut.

The nurse steps to within arm's length and runs a thermometer across my forehead. "Ninety-eight point six." She eyes me with suspicion and I read her thought: *Why are you here if you clearly don't have the Coronavirus?*

After a moment she asks the question aloud.

A wave a nausea washes over me. Speaking is more than I can manage, so I lean my head on David's shoulder and gently squeeze his arm. He begins explaining the situation to the nurse.

Her eyes shift back and forth between us, and she interrupts. "Is there a problem, that she can't answer for herself?"

The hand on my belly fists onto a wad of shirt and clenches. I raise my head and glower at her so hard my first words come out a snarl. "I'm. Sick." I collapse back onto David and manage to gasp out, "Autoimmune disorder."

The nurse makes the "Hmph" of disbelief but now I'm beyond caring. "Okay," she says, and I hear her eyes rolling in the words, "go in that door and they'll tell you what to do."

We turn to walk to that door and smug words follow. "Oh, not him. Only the patient can go in."

David walks me to the door anyway. I enter alone and another nurse, a tall dark woman with an interesting accent, asks my name, address, and birth date. I hand her my driver's license instead of answering. She types in the information, then asks, "Have you developed a recent cough or fever?"

"The nurse out there asked all the Covid screening questions," I say between deep breaths. "They're all *no*."

"It's protocol to ask again." Her answer is robotic. Of course everyone tells her they've already been asked. But then she seems to suddenly realize what I said. "All no? Then why do you think you have the virus?"

Why do I think…? Why does she think I think that? "I don't. I have a spondyloarthropathy—an autoimmune disorder that causes swollen joints, headaches, and an inflamed stomach. In an attack I throw up constantly and can't eat or drink for days. Now I'm so dehydrated, my blood pressure's dropping."

It takes two minutes to get those four sentences out. At the last one, the nurse eyes me sharply then grabs a cuff and slings it around my arm. After counting the beats she asks if I want a wheelchair.

"No, I can walk," I say, wondering how far and if I can really make it. She puts an arm under mine and helps me along, protocol evidently forgotten. Now we're getting somewhere.

Room. Gown. Bed. Sheet. She hands me the phone from my pants pocket and sets a cup of water on the table next to the bed. "Gary will be in to get your IV going in just a few minutes," she says as she walks out.

She pulls the door to but not closed and disappears. The uncovered window in the door is large enough to see that the three rooms across the foyer are empty even though all the lights outside of my room are dimmed. And the silence—you can tell when it's quiet not because people are asleep or hushed but because they're absent. That's the quality of this silence. I'm the only patient in this small wing.

I want to call David, but he worked hard all day and I told him to go get some rest. He probably isn't, but just in case I don't want to disturb him.

I try to nap. The bed is uncomfortable; I have to use my emesis bag and my head hurts; it's freezing; the light overhead is too bright; it's eerie being alone in an entire hospital wing. The dry air is making my parched throat even more scratchy so I call myself an idiot and put a few drops of water on my tongue to run down.

After a quarter hour I finally quit thinking about myself and turn my thoughts to the tens of thousands of Covid-19 victims lying alone in hospitals all over the world. Some elderly; others just children. Some will stay for days; others for weeks. What do I have to complain about? A couple hours and I'll be on my way home with my husband, hydrated and filled with powerful anti-nausea drugs. (I get to make this fun trip a couple times a year, so know what to expect.)

I text some colleagues so they know I won't be answering their emails tomorrow, zonked out in bed instead. Immediately my phone jumps with messages of well wishes. One special friend calls. We talk for more than forty minutes, during which time I thank god I let the drops of water run down my throat so I can control my voice. When I need to use the emesis bag, I tell her to hang on a sec and bury the phone in the covers and curse myself for letting water into my stomach.

When we hang up, I've been in this room well over an hour. In all that time, there hasn't been another person in the entire wing.

What if I had a real emergency? I'm not hooked to any machine; there wouldn't be any bells or alarms going off to alert a nurse somewhere. If I had a heart attack, or tried to get up and fell, no one would know until they got around to coming back. I don't know whether to be angry or frightened.

Gary finally shows up a full hour and twenty minutes after the nurse put me in here. I haven't seen a soul in all that time. "Sorry you had to wait," he says in a cheery voice that belies his words as he gathers the supplies for the IV. "People kept coming in to be tested, and if they screened positive we had to take care of them first. Now I'm going to draw a little blood and get you an IV going."

I try to make the words of his previous sentence mean something other than what he said. I can't, but maybe he misspoke.

"People were coming in that have coronavirus?" I look at the ceiling as I ask, because he's setting the needles out and I do better if I don't see them.

"We don't know. They came to get tested. They screen positive."

"But they're sick."

"We don't know." He speaks each word slowly, as if to a person just learning the language. Or stupid. "They came…"

"I mean, they're symptomatic?"

"Some of them, to varying degrees."

"But not all."

"No." He says this with hesitancy, by now figuring out that I'm going somewhere with this.

"But they still come first."

"That's the protocol." His voice is again cavalier, as though protocol makes everything right. The needle is in my vein and he pulls the tourniquet loose. The softness of skin brushing my arm shocks me and I glance down. He's not wearing gloves.

"So a non-symptomatic person who may not even be infected comes before the person having a heart attack or stroke, or bleeding out, or just really sick?" I thrust my full emesis bag at him, which is rude but I have no way to dispose of it, and I need to make this point: a pandemic does not mean every other disease has disappeared.

RAISING HELL
Bette J. Lafferty

Missed the marches
as I was ill.
The riots went unseen.

There's something to be said
   about
how being sick
can really do you in.

Screaming, chanting, doing
   harm,
what they did
was definitely wrong.

Their cause was just,
their actions not.
They numbered thousands
   strong.

Organized cells
across the states
knew their mission well.

Get the attention
of those in charge
by raising days of hell.

Violence hurt
the cause they sought,
destruction everywhere.

They burned their own.
Their brothers died.
The cost of change they'll bear.

Millions prayed,
forgiveness sought,
desiring peace once more.

Voices now heard,
discussions began
for ways to improve the score.

With shattered windows,
burning cars,
the crowds had lost control.

Still demands were made,
loopholes closed,
but change comes painfully slow.

BLOG WRITING DURING A PANDEMIC
Martha Slavin

As the sixth anniversary of writing my blog, "Postcards in the Air," drew closer, the world ceased to function normally. March 16, the date of Shelter In Place for the Bay Area, coincided with the starting date in 2014 of my first weekly blog posting.

During SIP, I began to notice patterns in writers the world over. Each week as I sat down to write my blog, I would try to find something that related to the pandemic as well as to my main topic of art and nature. So often after I finished my post, I would find an article or essay about the same topic. One week it was walking and observing more in nature, another week about decluttering, and further on, the emptiness of urban places. Just like me, writers expressed themes that SIP brought to their attention during each week. I marveled at how often my thoughts coincided with those of other writers.

In March, I wrote about how being an introvert made sequestering so much easier. I wrote about sheltering in place because I catch regular colds easily, let alone catching COVID19. I wrote about a squirrel building a nest and how nature ignored our travails. I wrote about first responders and neighbors who came forward. I wrote about how our society has forgotten the value of the common good. Each week, a different topic for me. Each week after I'd written my post, I would find articles on the same spectrum by other writers.

In April I pointed out how so many of us were tackling projects that needed to be done, such as cleaning out closets and reassessing our values. Or we had given in to the stress of the pandemic and found ourselves not able to do much at all. I used calligraphy to prompt people to think about the words, Remember, I Wish, and Together. I showed my husband's photos of our solitary walk around the eerily-empty San Ramon business park, where birds and ducks were flourishing, and humans had disappeared. I wrote about Earth Day and how the skies had cleared because of the lack of vehicles on the roads all over the world and how I hope we would learn something from the change.

In May I wrote about the effects of the sun, how humans need the sun, and how they were willing to break rules in order to be out at the beaches. During the month, I wrote about how everything mechanical was breaking in our house, how even inanimate objects seemed to be under stress. My husband Bill used his long-lost DIY skills, but some repairs needed experienced people. We worried about having other people in our home.

I wrote about an online class in making collages and how the practice of collage layering requires me to step back from the process and evaluate what I put down on paper. Each layer was a meditation about choices. I came back to writing about the wildlife that ventures into our yard in the spring. We have deer with new fawns and squirrels and birds making our yard their home.

And then George Floyd was murdered, and the world changed again. I asked myself if this was the time to write a blog about art and nature. I found myself delving into organizations that provide activism and support for the issues that Floyd's death brought up to our country. I found books to read and reminders that I needed to continue to be active and not put my blinders back on. Every essay that I read in the newspaper or online after I wrote mine had similar thoughts and calls for action.

Even three months into the pandemic, I was still not ready to return completely to my regular themes. I published an article about a small project that involves making art to express sorrow about deaths caused by gun violence. The Soul Box Project (SBP) collects origami boxes with the name of a person who has died from suicide, domestic violence, random or gang-related shootings, or from mass shootings. The project leaders are based in Portland and have exhibited as many as 15,000 boxes at various locations in Oregon. The exhibits heighten awareness of the numbers of people lost to gun violence.

In April 2021, the SBP plans to bring 200,000 boxes to the National Mall in Washington, D.C. The boxes remind me of the AIDS quilt project, which illustrates the power of something that starts small and grows in significance with each added creation. Again, I felt the universal pull to that idea. That week I got a notice from the Commonwealth Club that the AIDS quilt is coming back to San Francisco.

My sense of a collective consciousness with other writers seems to continue each week. Recently I finished my post about artists being agitators and gave the Che Guevara poster as an example. I turned off my computer and went to watch KQED, whose Canvas series that evening covered artists across the country making art to express their reactions to both the pandemic and Black Lives Matter movement.

We are in the middle of 2020, and I think back to January when I visited my eye doctor. He joked about the year, being full of good humor about 20/20. Though we haven't been able to joke much this year, 2020 has become a year of deep reflection and action towards more clarity in our beliefs and personal responsibilities. I think of myself as an independent person, thinking my own thoughts and writing them down as they come. It's only during a country-wide or world-wide event that I realize how close we all are in thought, how connected we all are, and that if we don't remember that connection we will be lost.

NOW I UNDERSTAND:
INSIGHT FROM COVID TIME
Jo Virgil

One thing that life has taught me is that even in what seems to be the toughest of times, good things can happen. And when they do, they provide a deeply meaningful lesson, one that is vital to carry inside forever. Paying attention to possibilities, though, matters.

When we had been under stay-at-home orders due to the COVID-19 pandemic for a few weeks and most of us were getting restless, anxious, and bored, one of my insightful friends came up with a great idea that would help. She posed a challenge for all of us, weather permitting, to walk around our neighborhood each day and take photos of interesting things, and then post those on Facebook for others to see. Of course, we knew to wear a face mask or practice social distancing, but the idea seemed like a perfect solution to the stress. Indeed, it is, but especially in a way I didn't foresee.

When I walk mindfully around my neighborhood, I spot things I hadn't noticed before—garden gnomes, welcome signs, beautiful flowers, silly statues, chalk messages on the sidewalks, puffy clouds, Buddha statues, painted rocks, even a longhorn cow—all sorts of things that make me smile. I take photos with my cell phone and share on Facebook almost every day. Friends love seeing the pictures, and some even got encouraged to do the same thing in their own neighborhoods.

But the even bigger gift came unexpectedly, like true gifts often do. In my walks around the hood, I would occasionally come across a neighbor I hadn't met before, outside doing yard work or getting into a car to drive off. Almost always we would chat for a few minutes, smile, and then move on. I'm sure that was nice for both of us. One encounter, though, profoundly changed my perspective on life.

I was walking down a street that I'd never been on before, many blocks from my home. I was checking out the houses as I walked by, looking for good photo-ops. Near the end of the street, I saw a man bringing out his trash bin to put out for curbside pick-up. When he turned to go back into his house, he spotted me and paused. I smiled and waved and walked a bit closer—still more than six feet apart, to be safe, but close enough to chat a bit. At first, he seemed a bit hesitant to visit, so I wasn't sure whether to just move on or not. But before I moved on, I pointed up to the sky to the rain clouds on the horizon moving our way. I told him that I was out walking early because the weather forecast was calling for rain that afternoon.

"You know, though, I'm never sure about those forecasts," I told him. Now he seemed more interested in listening. "I grew up in Amarillo. We had a TV weather forecaster who called himself Lyin' Dan the Weatherman, because he said even the professionals can't ever determine with absolute certainly what's going to happen."

That made him laugh, so we shared some chuckles there. Then he started chatting a bit more and shared some of the stories about strange weather he had seen in various places. Then we went on sharing a few other stories and we seemed, all of a sudden, to be good friends.

Did I mention that this man was Black? No, I didn't. To be honest, that didn't seem to matter until towards the end of our conversation. I just enjoyed chatting with him, and he had a great sense of humor and an open heart. But then I got to thinking about all the current Black Lives Matter protests, interviews, and news reports, raising our awareness of the still-existent racism problems, and the first thing I tied that to was this man's hesitation about talking to me at first. I am starting to realize, to a deeper degree, the subconscious anxiety that a Black person may feel when approached by a white stranger. The fact that we had such a fun conversation, though, erased that theme for both of us, it seems, at least temporarily. In fact, his parting words were what made my day, changed my life.

"I really enjoyed talking with you," he said as I waved goodbye. "Our conversation made my day so much brighter. I can't thank you enough."

That touched my heart in such a deep way. And our conversation made my day so much more insightful into a world I'd never thought enough about—the world of a Black person living in a time of still-existing racism. I will never forget that kind man, even if I don't cross paths with him ever again.

I wish that we didn't have to go through such trying times with the COVID-19 pandemic. But even in that darkness, there is light. There are lessons we can learn.

TIRED BUT NOT SICK
Patricia A. Dreyfus

If my mother were still alive, I'd ask her if her offer to slap me into next
    year is still on the table.
I am tired of 2020.
Tired of the negative politics;
tired of listening to politicians lie;
tired of Covid restrictions;
tired of seeing people gather without masks;
tired of them whining about their "rights;"
tired of being disappointed when Americans don't seem to care about
    others;
tired of watching grocery people, nurses, doctors, etc., work so hard
    with so little appreciation;
tired of people who think they know more than the experts;
tired of listening to people say "they" are coming to:
    1. rob their homes
    2. burn their boats
    3. take their children, jewels, way of life, etc.;
tired of those who forget we are all immigrants and yet took someone
    else's land and home;
tired of answering phone calls that tell me my friends are sick or dying.
I'm too tired to add all the rest. It's exhausting.
Will we learn from all this? Will we be a better nation? Will we be
    better individuals?
One friend says, "Let's celebrate New Year's Eve this Saturday, then the
    New Year, and get this *annus horribilis* over."
Good idea.
Now, I think I'll go take a long nap.

FIRE
Christa Pandey

It rages in the chest
from broken bones,
but those will calm and heal.
Not so the other fire,
flames of anger
high in city streets
for days and days.
The inequality,
systemic pressure
built up over centuries
is lapping at our democracy.

Unless we burn the hate to ashes,
revive the dream of a
"more perfect union"
from what is left
of goodwill and respect,
our country will go up in flames,
the sense of being special
killed by special forces,
new White House fences,
plastered with signs of protest.
Meanwhile the fortified
"cowardly lion" thinks he's safe.

Oh that we could light healing fires,
suffuse them with sage smudge, incense,
the flaming hearts of goodness,
the push of peaceful protests
crying out for change.

SARAH IN THE WINDOW
Elena Schwolsky

The bedroom window in the small apartment where Sarah Sharansky had lived for 25 years was the only window that looked out on the street. Sarah called it her window on the world. Before all this, when she was still leaving her apartment each day to teach English at the high school, Sarah looked out the window to see what people were wearing. When she saw open umbrellas, she grabbed hers from the flowered ceramic stand by the door.

She missed her walk to school, seeing her neighbor Emilio at his front gate, and his daily greeting, *"Hola Doña Sarah—como esta usted hoy?"*

Now she was the only one who could ask herself that question and she often did, aloud, as she started her day.

"How are you today, Sarah?" her voice scratchy from so little use.

It was the answer that was hard to figure out as days turned to weeks with no real end in sight, only a slow turning, full of uncertainty.

In the third week of the Stay-at-Home, it rained off and on, as if the weather was enforcing the order to stay inside. Sarah opened the shade to a view of the gray, wet street below—garbage bags still dotting the sidewalk, cars parked for weeks in the same spot. The rain created a dirt-streaked veil on the window through which she saw her narrow slice of the world.

The constant rain kept Sarah in bed longer each morning. Her days shifted from restless hours of making lists, emptying drawers, flinging clothes out of her overstuffed closet, to lethargic attempts to read, to write, or pick up the phone to call her longtime friend Nadine. In the last few days, her limbs had felt sodden, weighted down, as if they too had been absorbing the unceasing rain. Dragging her legs across the sheets took all the strength she had. Standing on what felt like two soggy tree trunks, she moved slowly to the window and opened the shade. Bright sunlight flooded the room. When had the rain stopped?

One lone yellow tulip had braved the chilly spring air in the small patch of garden in front of her building. The garbage was still piled by the curb and the cars were the same. But there were people on the street—Mrs. Santiago was standing on the stoop across the street, a man whose name she didn't know was walking a large German shepherd and a tiny chihuahua, a young boy hurrying by carried a grocery bag on each arm. They wore masks, they waved from a safe distance—but they were alive!

Of course, they were alive! It was then Sarah realized that she had been living as if the four walls of her isolated world, the rain, the virus, were all she would ever know again. She needed to shake off this gloomy outlook, but how?

How would she ever step back out into her city, into life?

———

Sarah heard them before she saw them from her usual spot at the window—the raggedy sound of voices shouting. The shouts turned into chants and she caught sight of one of the protests she had been watching on TV, coming right up her Brooklyn block. Thousands were gathering all across the country—the threat of the virus no match for their outrage.

The sound was muffled but she knew what they were shouting. Another unarmed black man had been killed by police. Sarah had marched through city streets herself once, though now, as the weeks turned into months, it seemed she could barely drag herself from the kitchen to the bedroom in her small apartment.

She peered through the window to the street below. They were still coming, moving up the block in waves.

Her eyes caught on one young woman, curly auburn hair flowing over her shoulders, head thrown back, a red bandana tied over her face. Sarah could imagine her mouth beneath her mask, twisted in pain and anger, pushing out the words

No Justice, No Peace.

The red-haired woman turned and looked up to the fifth floor where Sarah stood frozen in the window.

No Justice, No Peace!

She seemed to be sending her words right to Sarah.

An invitation.

Or maybe an accusation.

Sarah mouthed the words "I am with you" but the woman was gone, carried away by the sea of protesters and the power of their fury. Sarah retreated to her chair, listening as the last voices faded, as the street returned to its empty silence, and the sound of her own breath was the only thing she heard.

Sarah woke to the noise of the garbage truck on the street and shuffled her tired feet to the window. She had hardly slept. A few early shift workers were walking to the subway. Otherwise, the street was quiet.

Sarah hadn't turned off the TV till 3 AM, watching till all the protestors in Brooklyn, Minneapolis, and DC had gone home to get ready for another day.

"I feel so powerless, like a helpless old lady," she told Nadine. They had linked arms in many a protest march in their day.

"You've paid your dues, Sarah. You're entitled to rest," Nadine had said.

Sarah's friendship with Nadine had lasted decades, through lousy early marriages, through working together at the high school, through endless civil rights and anti-war meetings in damp church basements—their kids coloring together with broken crayons on the backs of old flyers.

That memory gave Sarah an idea. She rummaged in the closet and pulled out a piece of white posterboard she had shoved in there after she cleaned out her classroom. Her fingers raked through the junk drawer looking for a marker.

Sarah drew in big even letters—she hadn't been a teacher for nothing.

BLACK

LIVES

MATTER

And then she made the letters even thicker. She wanted people from across the street to see her sign, delivery people cruising down the block on electric bikes, dog walkers, the Fed Ex man. It was a small world she inhabited now, but she could do *something*.

She found some masking tape in the junk drawer and taped her sign in place in the window, then saluted it with a raised fist and spoke the words out loud.

BLACK LIVES MATTER!

Sarah giggled at the absurdity of her own private demonstration. There. She had done something. Not enough, but something.

Sarah studied her face in the rust-speckled mirror above the stained porcelain sink in her tiny bathroom. Were those new frown lines? She couldn't remember the last time she had smiled, really smiled. She smoothed her silver-grey hair, long grown out of its layered cut.

She had decided to leave her apartment, to walk up the block, to stand on her corner and join a vigil that some of her neighbors were organizing. She hadn't stepped over her worn marble threshold into the dimly lit hallway of her building since all of this began, more than three months ago.

It was time—time to venture out into the world. After watching on TV night after night—young people pouring into the streets in cities and towns all over the country—signs held high, voices full of emotion, faces streaked with tears—she had decided to join them.

She couldn't march but she would stand among them, 6 feet apart, with the purple cloth mask her neighbor, Mrs. Santiago, had hung over the doorknob for her. She had not yet worn it. Not even once.

She would bring the small brass bell she shook outside her window each night at 7 PM—thanking the workers.

She would offer her tired body and her heartbreak to those who were younger and stronger. She would let them know she saw them and heard them, feared for them and hoped for them. And she would pass the small flickering torch that she had kept burning inside her all these years, even when she didn't show it to anyone—she would pass that torch to them.

Sarah took a deep breath, adjusted the mask on her face, opened the door and stepped out into the world.

Time

LEARNING FROM COVID TIME
Jo Virgil

Humor and insight go hand-in-hand, it seems—
One to lift the spirit, the other to open its door,
To let the light shine through in colorful beams,
Allowing Truth to shine through its core.

The COVID-19 lock-down has shattered many dreams,
Awakened us from "normal" and pushed us into Now,
Causing us to take some time to figure what this all means,
Pushing us to examine life—who, what, when, where, how.

I came up with my own approach that made my friends all laugh:
Dos XX Therapy, I say—some beer and contemplation,
Sitting quietly on my porch, being with all of nature, not half,
And pondering the whole world, not just my one nation.

The more I pause and look outside myself,
The more I feel connected and the more peace I find.
This pandemic is not only about our health,
It's about connecting our souls, our hearts, and our minds.

SILVER LINING
Jane Gragg Lewis

Growing up, I always heard that every cloud has a silver lining. I imagine most everyone – no matter the language or the country – has heard this thought expressed in one way or another.

Listening to the news, I don't think any fear-mongering news casters want to look for silver now that the world has started taking Covid-19 seriously and all has gone topsy-turvey. Just panic-gendering doom and gloom is what is broadcast 24/7.

California was way ahead of other states and locked down tight – and then tighter. Signs posted everywhere with lots "don'ts" and no "dos" are generating comments and bad jokes about living in a police state. Every day, there are more ugly numbers to report.

And then…one bright morning on one of my almost-daily bike rides through fields flooded with wild daisies, I see something that makes me pull my bike to the side of the trail and stop to watch. I smile as I see a young, working-from-home, or maybe out-of-work, father kneel beside the trail in front of a stroller. He's carefully picking wild daisies for his little jogging buddy, while she patiently supervises. As he presents the wonderfully wild bouquet to her, she rewards him with squeals of delight and his face glows.

Finally, there it is: that promised glint of silver, lining the fluff of white in the cobalt sky above us. The gift of time.

Fast Forward to the Year 2040

Sera was the little girl in that stroller, four years old at the time. A woman that day told her that she would always remember that bouquet of yellow and white daisies. Today, she and her boyfriend went on a hike. He picked wild daisies for her and she smiled.

A smile of remembrance.

THE DISCOVERY
Bette J. Lafferty

Days of Sheltered in Place proved
a perfect time to clean an accumulation
of papers, articles, and stories written,
hiding in the back of my closet.

Years of memories logged in Weekly Planners,
Day-Timers and Appointment Books used as
journals revealed my life one page at a time.
Pile after pile required careful attention to words
and thoughts important at the time; many relevant
even for today.

The final box, filled to the brim with what some
call clutter, revealed a file of old love letters.
One by one, I read the words that flew off

the pages tugging at my heart. Such fresh
love sent my mind spinning. What exciting
carefree times reclaimed.

The words *I Love You* filled page after page
written by a man that seldom verbalized such
desire. Tears streamed down my face as I
drank in the passion our young love held.

Oh, to go back and relive those days again…
and yet, I realize they were only for a season.
Thankful for each memory, each letter, each
word of love etched on paper now yellowing
with time.

Blessed beyond my wildest dreams, I realize
many never experience such tenderness
shared, or such intimacy offered. Total
abandonment of self, relinquishing all
control and expectations only to love and
to be loved.

A gift, a memory that comes once in a lifetime,
sealed with undying love which was almost lost
in the removal of clutter. I remain forever
thankful for the days Sheltering in Place.

THEIR PECULIAR WAYS
Sara Etgen-Baker

"Wash your hands, little lady!"

"I already washed them just a little while ago. Why should I wash them again?"

"You've touched countless things since then; your hands are dirty."

"But Grammy," I turned my hands over, closely examining them. "They don't look dirty!"

"Yes, they are! The kind of dirt I'm talking about is invisible; it rides on your hands and can make you sick. It can only be removed with soap and water. So go wash your hands!"

Invisible dirt riding on my hands? I hadn't heard of such a thing and didn't understand why I washed my hands more at Grammy's house than I did at home. *Maybe she has more invisible dirt at her house,* I speculated. Grammy had many other peculiar ways so I chalked up her hand washing practice as another one of them.

Before the advent of disinfecting wipes and hand sanitizer, Grammy took sheets of paper towel and a small can of disinfecting spray with her wherever she went, stuffing them inside her rather spacious purse. While out and about, she used her spray, liberally coating the surface of restaurant tables, public phones, restroom door knobs, etc., then vigorously rubbing the area with a paper towel until the coating disappeared. Although I didn't understand her obsession and found her ritual odd, irritating, and even a little embarrassing, I never asked her why she did what she did. Perhaps I should've. Instead, I dismissed her habits as silly. *Just another one of Grammy's peculiar ways,* I reasoned.

Even my mother had her own baffling ways. She didn't use her dishwasher because it cost too much to run. She always darned our socks; fashioned quilts from the clothes I outgrew; made cleaning rags out of worn-out towels; and never threw away any empty plastic butter tubs. Instead, she washed them and stored them in a kitchen cabinet for putting leftovers in. When I questioned her about it, she said, "No need to spend money on fancy store-bought plastic storage when I already have plastic." Much to my dismay, the cabinet frequently became so full that when I opened the door, butter tubs tumbled out and onto the kitchen floor next to my feet.

Bar soap was cheaper than body wash or liquid hand soap and was, therefore, Mother's preferred choice for washing one's hands and body. Anyone who's ever used bar soap knows that the bar gets smaller and smaller with each use. Eventually, all that remains is a balled up, dirty, disfigured, and insignificant piece of soap that's annoyingly impossible to use. Mother habitually gathered up all those mutant miniature soaps and placed them in—you guessed it—the empty butter tubs. Once she'd collected enough tiny soap pieces, she chopped them up, placed them in a Styrofoam cup, filled it with water, and cooked it in the microwave for 30 seconds. After drying for a few days, wah-la! A new bar of soap. Even as baffling as Mother's idiosyncrasies were, I never thought to ask her why she did what she did. I simply laughed to myself and dismissed her, *Such an odd woman!*

So what's the point of rambling on about these women's peculiar ways? Because I later learned their *why.* Grammy was 18 when the 1918 flu pandemic began, and she lost a cousin to the virus. During that pandemic, she volunteered at a local hospital, making her highly sensitized to the presence of unseen germs. Mother grew up during the Great Depression. Due to high prices, low incomes, and high demand, the government instituted rationing. Sugar, coffee, meat, fish, butter, eggs, and cheese were rationed to prevent hording, prepare for war efforts, and insure most people had at least a little food. Out of necessity, Mother learned to live prudently and waste nothing.

I, on the other hand, grew up in a bountiful time, lived in a disposable society filled with every convenience imaginable, and hadn't ever had to deal with a global calamity as my grandmother and mother had. But when the COVID-19 pandemic struck, my world and life as I knew it changed seemingly overnight. Suddenly I had a new appreciation for what I thought were Grammy's over-the-top sanitizing habits. When store shelves emptied in the wake of the current pandemic, I found myself understanding Mother's fear of not having, and respecting her frugality.

I realized that their ways were not at all peculiar. Rather, their ways were seasoned in their life experiences and came from living during a calamity like a global pandemic, war, and an economic depression. These were life-altering experiences in which they adapted and created habits, mindsets, and responses that stayed with them throughout their lives.

This pandemic has impacted me in much the same way. I've developed new habits: like washing my hands more frequently, removing what Grammy called *invisible dirt*; carrying disinfecting wipes and a mask in my purse; using fewer paper towels; using bar soap instead of liquid soap; using less laundry detergent; eating smaller portions; and generally living more prudently. With sheltering in place, I've slowed down, shut out the noise, and gone inward. Although I haven't begun darning socks, saving butter tubs, or making soap, I've become aware of how quickly I sometimes judge or ridicule another person's actions because I didn't know or even acknowledge that person might have a backstory that shaped them and their responses to life itself.

My erroneous thinking has given me pause, and now I'm consciously waiting before rushing to judge so that I might acknowledge a person's life circumstances are different from mine and respect those differences even if I don't understand them. I'm transitioning into a more mindful and tolerant person – a wonderful, unexpected byproduct of the pandemic. I'm reminded of my mother's wise words: "Calamity is a great teacher. Within it are the seeds of change."

WE THE PEOPLE
Christa Pandey

For years the country
did not feel united,
was told that we were red or blue.
Then came the COVID scourge
with social distancing
and orders to stay home.

But a few months into it
technology devised a miracle
that brought unlikely folks together
by zoom or other electronic means.
From far and wide across the continent
people converged in virtual meetings,
made decisions, shared ideas,
conjured musical events, where choirs
and orchestras, though each

at home, performed their parts,
an unimagined new experience.

A highlight of this new technology
was on display at the big Dem convention,
where children from all fifty states
sang out in unison, but from their homes,
the US national anthem.
Their t-shirts red and white and blue,
but more importantly their faces
black and white and brown of shades
that for Crayola would be hard to replicate,
gave proof of our diversity
as rarely seen, much less perceived.

Next day the "roll call" tabulating
votes for the presumptive nominee,
in normal years a boring exercise
of silly hats and boastful shouting,
became a highlight as each delegation
stood in their own state, showcasing
a day in history, a product, prominence.
Hawaiian beaches, Midwest corn,
Rhode Island calamari,
the Selma Pettus bridge,
the Oklahoma massacre,
Michigan's car industry,
and many health providers
pleading still for PPE.

We only witnessed it on TV,
but had a sense of unity, belonging,
that yes, THIS is our country, and
"we the people" still has currency.

DEAR CORONA
Jude Walsh

As the world economy shut down, amidst the sickness and death, the earth began to heal itself, everyday heroes stepped up, and creativity unfurled in unexpected ways. I wanted to explore my feelings about and connection with this virus so I decided to write to it directly.

April 27, 2020

Dear Corona,

Is it weird that I want to first thank you? Our world is in the midst of a huge shift, a huge reset, initiated by you. There is much talk about you as an enemy that must be defeated, that we are at war against you. I wish we could shift perspective and consider working with you, for the good of all.

What causes many of us the most distress is the sickness and suffering. Some people who have the virus interact with you quite dramatically. Others struggle very little. Some seem to not even be aware you were part of them. And then of course there are the deaths. Since my son Bren died, I have shifted in my feelings about dying. It sounds "new-age-y" but I now see it as transitioning. Once I knew that, my sympathy moved more toward the living who have lost loved ones, knowing the adjustment for them is more difficult. That many people pass without family or friends at their side is particularly painful.

I am deeply distressed by the toll this is taking on the caregivers. The medical, custodial, clerical, first responders, food service, pharmacy workers, etc., who are on the frontlines, either caring for the sick or helping those of us who are isolated still get our basic needs met. I am so grateful to them. Can you go easy on them please?

I am concerned about the stress of isolation, both for those alone and for those in constant contact. I am concerned about those in abusive or other way dangerous settings; this increases their peril.

Of course the economy is an issue. But it is not just a problem for us here in the United States. The world economy is collapsing in dire ways. What does this mean? My parents survived The Depression. It forever affected their sense of safety and the way they responded to and cared for money and possessions. I believe I acquired some of their perspective through DNA and got the rest via their words and example.

I also inherited their grit. My impulse is to dig in, persevere, help those I can, pray for everyone, and try and spread hope, healing, and beauty to the best of my ability.

I am heartened by the speed of healing in our environment. After just a few weeks of pause, we have cleaner air and water, bluer skies, more relaxed animals, more life! We are all longing to be outside and experience this firsthand. Can we find a way to continue to keep our air and water clean as we return to "business?"

I am heartened by the contacts we are making via the Internet. Perhaps this is the lesson we have long needed, how to connect *emotionally* online and not just for communication and business. Despite all the criticism of Facebook, at this moment thousands are interacting with people they have not thought about in years, having a little time and Internet access and using the search engine to reconnect.

As a creative, as a writer, as a music and art lover, what is most encouraging is the explosion of creativity. It makes me weep at the beauty of it all. Perhaps one day what was begun now and later enhanced will be known as the Corona Renaissance Period.

Your greatest lesson to us is about borders. As a virus, it is of no interest to you whatsoever that if you cross some line you are now in another country. Like wind and weather you go where you will. Those borders are arbitrary. Perhaps for us to coexist with you in peace, we need to accept and work with this. It is my prayer and deepest desire that we unite at a global level to make things better for all, not just for the USA.

So, while much suffering has ensued, perhaps many blessings are forthcoming. Am I lonely? Yes. Am I learning? Yes. Do I want to be more in the world? Yes. Am I willing to wait, be patient, until the lessons are learned and assimilated? Sigh, yes. Am I crabby and frustrated sometimes? Yes. Am I willing to do my part to help with the healing? Yes. Am I grateful? Yes.

Corona, you swept in wildly. Perhaps you can calm yourself. Perhaps you can show us how to live with you in harmony. Perhaps we can learn to live in harmony with one another.

Let us hope.
XO

Jude

BEATITUDES IN THE TIME OF PANDEMIC
Catherine Johnson

Blessed are the doctors and nurses making do with so little, working endlessly long shifts, and at the end of the day, wondering what they carry home. And, the environmental service workers, who clean up the mess, and strip the beds of the dead; theirs will surely be the kingdom of heaven.

Blessed be the leaders, the wise and the humble, the arrogant and the stupid, someday they will be separated, like wheat from the chaff, and after that, only God knows; may their mercy be just and granted.

Blessed be those in detention, the incarcerated, and the held, for they have practiced isolation and loneliness, learned patience and fortitude; may they be granted sweet release.

Blessed be those who keep showing up, the stockers and checkers, butchers and baggers, farmers and fishers, drivers and boxers; may theirs be a rich reward.

Blessed be the parents who reassure their children, though their own confidence be shaken and small; may they know peace and easy play, once again.

Blessed be the homeless, without shelter or food; may they be comforted and fed.

Blessed be the elderly, the vulnerable, and frail; may they be granted tenderness and care.

Blessed be the whole world in this ravaged time, the ones who sing from their balconies, who say their last goodbye, who pray and who mourn, who make beauty, who weep, who marvel in wonder, who are generous and gentle, who do what they can; may they all know the kindness of God.

A Transformation

THE NEW DAWN, BETA, AND A DEEP BREATH
Susan Wittig Albert

The summer was brutal, and my New Dawn rose, a quarter-century old, was showing the effects. In early September, when I finally paused to take a look at it, all I could see was a mass of lifeless, leafless brown sticks threaded through the trellis. This was a first, for over the 25 years of its life, this resilient antique rose, known for its hardiness, had never lost its green leaves until winter, with its persistent killing frosts.

But August's blistering string of rain-free 100-degree-plus days had been too much for even the New Dawn, and I hadn't helped. It had been a long, brutal Covid-fueled summer, and—like the rest of us in this crazy year—I had all I could do just to keep things together. I took the rose for granted. I thought it didn't need me, that it could survive and even flourish without me. I didn't recognize the danger until Labor Day, when I walked out on the deck and suddenly saw that the rose was leafless and brown. Why hadn't I watered it? My inattention had killed it. I felt terrible. That rose was as hardy as they come. I count on its lush, luxuriant greenness to fill an important place at the side of the deck. How had I been so negligent, so inattentive, so care/less? I got out the hose, but I knew it was too little, too late. Much too late.

And then tropical storm Beta blew in off the Gulf, dumping a deluge of flooding rain on the Texas Coastal Bend and across five other states. It was an ugly storm, killing at least two and flooding thousands of homes. Here in the Hill Country, 200 miles inland, we got barely an inch over a couple of days, but it came with a blessed cool-down. And just a day or two after Beta had spiraled off to the northeast, the New Dawn put out a sudden flush of eager green leaves. The bush has been seriously damaged, I'm sure, but its revival felt like a miracle. It *was* a miracle, far as I was concerned.

Nature is always teaching us something. The rose reminds me that the world we know and love is bravely resilient – but also frighteningly vulnerable. Beta is another demonstration of the truth that what's damaging, even deadly, for some can be beneficial, even hope-filled, for others. The episode warns me that I need to be more attentive to what's happening around me, less negligent. I must care more, be more watchful.

And I have to learn that I can't count on miracles. The name "Beta" tells me that it's already been a very long hurricane season – and there are two more months (and another whole alphabet) to go. The disastrous fires on the West Coast remind me that climate change can be irrevocable. The designation "Covid-19" carries the warning that there can be a Covid-21 or -22, with even more dire impact. Throughout this Covid year, the reliability and accessibility of our health care system, the impartiality of our judicial system, and even the integrity of our electoral system – all have been under attack. I have felt that our *democracy* is under attack. This year was my eighty-first on this planet, and I have never, ever felt so vulnerable.

But back to roses and storms. I am grateful to West Coast friends Christina Baldwin and Ann Linnea, who recently wrote this in their Peer Sprit newsletter: "The smoke was an event. The fires are a disaster. What we're living through is a transformation. It's not going to 'get over with' and return us to the old status quo. Like a burned forest, life will return—but it will not be the same forest. We are in it now, the big turn, the long work, the unraveling and reweaving. Whenever you can, take a deep breath."

I'm taking a deep breath. It won't be the same forest, no. It will be the big turn and the long work, yes. But October is here, with its blessed crisp mornings. November will bring the election and its aftermath. December will take us into the quiet darkness of winter. And then will come January, with its many new beginnings – its promises of hope and fairness and justice, for *all.*

A deep breath, a big turn, the long work. And my own pledge to work harder, pay more attention, take more responsibility. And be a part of the unraveling and the reweaving.

ABOUT THE CONTRIBUTORS

SUSAN WITTIG ALBERT – BERTRAM TX

Susan Wittig Albert is the author of books for young readers, mysteries and biographical fiction for adults, and memoir and nonfiction. In 1997, she founded the Story Circle Network to embody her passion for women's stories. A mother, grandmother, and great-grandmother, she lives with her husband Bill in the Texas Hill Country. https://susanalbert.com

JUDY ALTER – FORT WORTH TX

Award-winning Texas author Judy Alter tells the stories of women in the nineteenth-century American West and writes contemporary mysteries. She is the author of over a hundred books, essays, book reviews, columns, and cookbooks. The mother of four and grandmother of seven, she is retired as director of TCU Press and lives in a wonderful cottage in Fort Worth with her dog, Sophie. http://www.judyalter.com

MARIAN L. BEAMAN – JACKSONVILLE FL

Marian Longenecker Beaman is a former professor at Florida State College in Jacksonville, Florida. Her memoir, Mennonite Daughter: The Story of a Plain Girl, records the charms and challenges of growing up in the strict culture of the Lancaster Mennonite Conference in the 1950s and '60s. The author writes weekly on her blog: https://marianbeaman.com. She lives with her artist husband Cliff in Florida, where her grown children and grandchildren also reside.

DEBORAH L. BEAN – ROWLETT TX

A native Texan, Deborah L. Bean was raised during the height of the moon race, which piqued her interest in science fiction from a young age. In 2016, she completed her Graduate Certificate in the "Your Novel Year" program from ASU. She has had user manuals, Sci-fi and fantasy stories, and memoir pieces published during her career, including by the Story Circle Journal, the Writers Guild of Texas, and WordWare Publishing.

JOYCE BOATRIGHT – HUNTSVILLE TX

Joyce Boatright is a writer, storyteller, and workshop leader. Her book, Haikus for the Soul, is scheduled for release in 2021. http://www.JoyceBoatright.com

CLAIRE BUTLER – CINCINNATI OH

I hail from Cincinnati, and have two non-fiction manuscripts nearly ready for release. I am a writer and an artist, painting oil on canvas. I have been published in several journals and one anthology, and have been selling my art since 2007. My two fur babies, Tilly and Gigi, are always at my feet whether at the computer or the easel. http://www. Claire-Butler.com

ANTOINETTE CARONE – NEW YORK NY

Antoinette Carone is a member of the New York Writers' Coalition and The Italian American Writers' Association. She has published a journal, *Ciao, Napoli,* as well as *A Scrapbook of Wandering in Naples,* and a short story collection, *Siren Shore—the Enchantment of Naples.* Her short stories have appeared in O "The Eternal Return" appeared in *Ovunque Siamo* in May 2018, and "The Demon" in January 2019. "Appearance" appeared in *Foxglove Journal* in January 2020. Her website is https://italianscrapbook.wordpress.com.

JULIE CHAVEZ – PLEASANTON CA

Julie Chavez is a writer and a peddler of library books in Northern California. She's been blogging at www.25000words.com since 2012 and recently completed her first memoir.

SUSAN D. CORBIN – AUSTIN TX

Susan D. Corbin graduated from the University of Texas with a doctorate in Communication Studies. Currently, she lives in Austin with her husband of 48 years and their dog, Sadi. Her essays have been published by Story Circle Network. Other projects include a book called *Dear Dissertation Writer: Get your Dissertation Done and Stay Sane* and a memoir about her granddaughter's heart transplant at ten months old, tentatively titled *Evie's Heart.* https:// corbindissertationcoaching.com

HENDRIKA DE VRIES – SANTA BARBARA CA

Hendrika de Vries is the author of *When a Toy Dog Became a Wolf and the Moon Broke Curfew,* a memoir about her childhood in Nazi-occupied Amsterdam that won the 2019 Sarton Women's Book Award. A depth-oriented family therapist for over thirty years, she used memory, intuitive imagination and dreams to heal trauma and empower women. As faculty at Pacific Graduate Institute, she helped students explore their archetypal life patterns. She lives in Santa Barbara. Her website is: http://www.agirlfromamsterdam.com/

DEBRA DOLAN – VANCOUVER BC CANADA

Debra Dolan lives on the west coast of Canada, where she enjoys long solitary walks, reading memoir, deep conversations over red wine, and chronicling daily life's myriad of joys and challenges. After many wonderful years in Vancouver, she is spending the winter transitioning to life in a small funky town high in the mountains, where she welcomes new connections and a spontaneous active life.

PATRICIA DREYFUS – CORONA DEL MAR CA

Patricia Dreyfus is published in *The Best Travel Writing, Los Angeles Times, Daily Pilot, She Writes Anthology, Three Minus One, Twins Magazine,* and *The California Quarterly.* Her nearly finished memoir is *Woman-Be Quiet.* Patricia is a member of The Writing Well, PEN, Greater Los Angeles Writers Society, Academy of American Poets, LA Poets-Writers Collective, AWP, California State Poetry Society, Amherst Writers, IWWG, Story Circle Network, The Thursday Writers Critique, Women Writing the West. She edited the book *13 Weeks.* http://patriciadreyfus-writer.com/

SARA ETGEN-BAKER – ANNA TX

A teacher's unexpected whisper, "You've got writing talent," ignited Sara's writing desire. Sara ignored that whisper and pursued a different career, but eventually she rediscovered her inner writer and began writing. Her manuscripts have been published in anthologies and magazines including *Chicken Soup for the Soul,* Guideposts, *Times They Were A-Changing,* and *Wisdom Has a Voice.*

D FERRARA – WYCKOFF NJ

D Ferrara is a writer, collaborator, and editor of *American Writers Review* and *Art in the Time of COVID-19.* She has published numerous stories, articles, essays and reviews, and considers membership in Story Circle Network an honor and a privilege.

SARAH FINE – TORONTO ON CANADA

I am a mostly unpublished writer and poet, born and raised in Canada from colonizer and Indigenous ancestry, living most of my life in Toronto on the shores of Lake Ontario, an environmentalist and a lover of trees, a Baby Boomer mother of three adult children, a wife for 36 years, a retired introvert and an optimist.

LAURA MAURER GOODELL, MD – AUSTIN TX

Laura is a wife, mother of four, sister, daughter, aunt, niece, cousin, in-law, friend, physician, dog owner, walker, runner, reader, writer, cook, dishwasher, suburban dweller, cleaner of the house, scrubber of the kitchen, homeschooler, living in the pandemic in Austin. Laura used to be a traveler. When she sits in her backyard, she often thinks of places to go, but she realizes she is right where she needs to be.

B. LYNN GOODWIN – DANVILLE CA

Lynn Goodwin owns Writer Advice, www.writeradvice. com. She's written *Never Too Late: From Wannabe to Wife at 62* (memoir), *Talent* (YA) and *You Want Me to Do WHAT? Journaling for Caregivers* (self-help). *Never Too Late* and *Talent* are multiple award-winners. Shorter works ran in Hip Mama, The Sun, Dramatics Magazine, Good Housekeeping, Purple Clover, and Flashquake. A reviewer and teacher at Story Circle Network, she lives at the foot of Mt. Diablo with her energizer-bunny husband and exceptional terrier.

JEANNE BAKER GUY – CEDAR PARK TX

Jeanne Guy, author, speaker, journal-writing coach, lives in Texas with her architect-husband and two spoiled cats. She's known for her "Re-Story" journaling workshops, helping people reframe their inner narrative. Jeanne co-authored *Seeing Me: a guide to reframing the way you see yourself.* Her memoir, *You'll Never Find Us*, the story of how her children were stolen from her and how she stole them back, is scheduled for 2021 publication by She Writes Press. She writes irreverent blogs. Her website, http://www.jeanneguy.com/, needs a doctor.

ANN HAAS – MOGADORE OH

I am a certified legacy writer/facilitator, who has taught legacy writing at the local, state and national levels including training Family Practice residents at my local hospital. I established the legacy program at my local hospice and developed legacy writing tools for the memory impaired. My legacy writing specialties are blessings, six-word memoirs, reverse bucket lists, *au plein air* nature writing and a storytelling method using a three-question memoir format.

LINDA HOYE – KAMLOOPS BC CANADA

Linda Hoye lives in British Columbia with her husband and their doted-upon Yorkshire Terrier, but will always be a Saskatchewan prairie girl. She is the author of *The Presence of Absence: A Story About Busyness, Brokenness, and Being Beloved* and *Two Hearts: An Adoptee's Journey Through Grief to Gratitude*. Find her online at www. lindahoye.com where she ponders ordinary days and the thin places where faith intersects.

CATHERINE JOHNSON – VASHON WA

Catherine Johnson lives, writes, and farms with her wife of 30 years on Vashon Island in Washington. Her essays and poems have appeared in the following anthologies: *The Nature of an Island, Scent of Cedars, Secret Histories, Face to Face: Women Writers on Faith, Mysticism and Awakening,* and *The Weird World Rolls On.* Her memoir, *Finding Mercy In This World,* received the 2018 Sarton Women's Book Award. Currently, she is working on a new collection of poems.

NIRMALA KSHATRIYA – SANTA CLARA CA

Nirmala Kshatriya is a bilingual author, who has been published in English and Hindi for the last 50 years. Her articles on parenting have been published in Femina, and works on Indian freedom fighters in the Hindi journal, Dharmyug. She wrote a column on Dream Interpretation for The Times of India. After being widowed in 2012, Nirmala moved from Bangalore to the US to be with her three children in the San Francisco Bay Area.

BETTE J. LAFFERTY – BOERNE TX

Bette moved from Florida to Texas Hill Country at age 82, when her son decided she needed to live closer to him. Widowed in 2010, Bette began writing seriously, and became an award-winning poet with the National League of American Pen Women. She sends out her writings under the title of Monday Morning Offerings to 165 readers. Her joy is to share the love of Jesus. Bette enjoys reading, her small flower garden, and life in general.

JANE GRAGG LEWIS – LAGUNA NIGUEL CA

Jane Gragg Lewis lives in Southern California, where she enjoys the near-perfect weather riding her bike, playing Pickleball, or visiting the San Diego Zoo/Safari Park. She has published two books: an ESL activity text, *Dictation Riddles*; and a memoir, *A Jar of Fireflies*.

TERI LIPTAK – TYLER TX

Teri Liptak lives in Texas with her supportive husband, Eric, two opinionated cats, and one loud-mouthed dachshund. Her son, Logan, and daughter-in-law, Kasey, also live in Texas and keep her inspired. After experiencing "empty nest syndrome" and more free time than she was used to, Teri began exploring writing and art. She enjoys writing women's literary fiction and poetry. Currently, she's working on a novel-length story. You can follow her at Twitter: https://twitter.com/teriliptak

TERESA LYNN – GEORGETOWN TX

Teresa Lynn has written for a range of publications on a variety of topics and has authored three books. In 2014, she established Tranquility Press, where she provides all types of editorial and publishing services. She is also administrator and a board member of SCN and president of ACFW Cen-Tex. Teresa speaks to groups nationwide on select subjects. See her website at: http://www.henscratches.com/

BETTY MCCREARY – AUSTIN TX

I am a nature lover and bird watcher. I was born in Austin and live here with my husband, two dogs, and one cat. Our three kids are grown and on their own. I belong to a women's life writing group and a fiction group. We have continued our writing together through Zoom meetings and miss hugging each other. Blog: https://naturalmusings.blog

MERIMÉE MOFFITT – ALBUQUERQUE NM

Merimée retired from teaching to focus on her writing and has published five books since 2013 (two reviews on Story Circle Book Reviews). She has been a teacher for SCN and several times a judge in the annual contests. She has participated in community workshops, teaching here and there in Albuquerque, a city with a high per capita rate of poets and happy roadrunners enjoying the lack of traffic. http://www.merimeemoffitt.com

TRACIE NICHOLS – LANSDALE PA

Tracie Nichols, M.A., is a poet exploring human and wild nature through words, making sense of a world that feels both intriguing and often overwhelming. She regularly contributes to KindOverMatter. com and Journey of the Heart: Women's Spiritual Poetry Project. So far, her work has appeared in three anthologies of women's poetry.

Tracie lives under rustling trees in southeastern Pennsylvania with her husband, a very determined ginger tabby cat, Strider, and, for an unexpected moment, her three adult children.

CHRISTA PANDEY – AUSTIN TX

Christa Pandey is an Austin poet, who has published four chapbooks: Southern Seasons, Maya, Hummingbird Wings, Who am I? Who are We? Many of her single poems have appeared in journals (online and in print) and anthologies. Lately she has concentrated on haiku and senryu as the ultimate compression of words. http://karmawings.wordpress.com

MARILEA RABASA – CAMANO ISLAND WA

Marilea Rabasa is a retired ESL teacher and the award-winning author of her first memoir, *A Mother's Story: Angie Doesn't Live Here Anymore.* Her sequel memoir, *Stepping Stones*, was published in June 2020, and was a Finalist in the 2020 IBA awards. Her recovery blog is: www.recoveryofthespirit.com. She and her partner moved permanently to the Pacific Northwest recently. Summers are for grandchildren and salt air at their home on an island in Puget Sound.

CHRISTINE RISTAINO – SCOTTDALE GA

Christine Ristaino is an Atlanta author, whose memoir, *All the Silent Spaces*, has earned numerous book awards in the categories of Inspirational Memoir, Social Change, and Women's Issues. Her book confronts the topics of discrimination and overcoming violence. In addition, Ristaino has published articles in the Guardian, Pacific Standard, the Washington Post, the Huffington Post, and the Atlanta Journal-Constitution on child advocacy, coping with violence, and diversity. Ristaino is also an award-winning advisor and teacher. www.christineristaino.com

KALÍ ROURKE – AUSTIN TX

Kalí Rourke is a full-time philanthropist and volunteer in the Austin area, and has lent her writing, public speaking, and social media skills to many local nonprofits, including Story Circle Network. She is a wife, mom, singer, and an advocate for mentoring in all of its forms. https://kalipr.wordpress.com/

EILEEN HARRISON SANCHEZ – SOUTH PLAINFIELD NJ

Eileen Harrison Sanchez is now retired after a forty-year career in education. She started as a teacher and ended as a district administrator. Eileen is a member of the Historical Novel Society, Goodreads American Historical Novels Group, Philadelphia Stories Writers Community, and several online writers' groups. A reader, a writer, and a perennial—a person with a no-age mindset—she considers family and friends to be the most important parts of her life, followed by traveling and bird watching from her gazebo. https://eileensanchez.com

ELENA SCHWOLSKY – BROOKLYN NY

Elena Schwolsky is a nurse, community health educator, activist, and writer. Her award-winning memoir, *Waking in Havana: A Memoir of AIDS and Healing in Cuba* was published in November 2019 by She Writes Press. Her work has also been included in the anthologies *Storied Dishes: What Our Family Recipes Tell Us About Who We Are and Where We've Been* and *Reflections on Nursing: 80 inspiring stories on the art and science of nursing.* http://www.elenaschwolsky.com

LISA A. SEEL – ALLISON PARK PA

Lisa Seel is a wife, mother, sister, and daughter living in Pittsburgh, Pennsylvania. In addition to writing, her passions are cooking, crafting, reading, and spending time with friends and family. After retiring from her elementary school teaching position, Lisa helped to imagine, establish, and open the Millvale Community Library, a small public library in a neighborhood of Pittsburgh. Today she runs the writing group that meets there.

MADELINE SHARPLES – MANHATTAN BEACH CA

Madeline Sharples authored *Papa's Shoes: A Polish shoemaker and his family settle in small-town America* (historical fiction published by Aberdeen Bay), as well as a memoir in prose and poetry, *Leaving the Hall Light On: A Mother's Memoir of Living with Her Son's Bipolar Disorder and Surviving His Suicide*, and *Blue-Collar Women: Trailblazing Women Take on Men-Only Jobs*. She co-edited *The Great American Poetry Show* anthology and wrote the poems for *The Emerging Goddess* photograph book. Her poems have appeared online and in print. http://madelinesharples.com

C.V. SHAW – MIAMI FL

C.V. Shaw is the author behind *The Spell*. She is a Doctor of Oriental Medicine and a Quantum Energy Practitioner and instructor. She is a native South Floridian and holds her alternative medicine practice out of South Miami. She has published work in *How to Survive your Teenager*. Previously a journalist, she was a feature writer for M.D. News, Florida Medical Business, Miami Herald Neighbors, and Club Systems International. https://cvshawbooks.com

MARTHA SLAVIN – DANVILLE CA

Martha Slavin is an artist and writer. Her blog, *Postcards in the Air*, can be found each Friday at http://www.marthaslavin.blogspot.com. Martha paints using water-based media, crafts collages, creates artist's books, is a printmaker and calligrapher. She writes poetry and personal essays. Her essays have appeared in two anthologies, *Something That Matters* and *Wednesday Writers*. Her artwork has appeared in Cloth Paper Scissors magazine and Stampington's Somerset Studio magazine. She has exhibited at numerous California galleries.

JOAN STEVENSON – LAFAYETTE CA

When I retired years ago, I wondered how to answer when asked, "What do you do?" Now I boldly declare myself a writer. When you are 86 years old you can do that. I have written and published first-person columns for the newspapers in the San Francisco Bay area since I retired twenty years ago. I am passionate about giving women a voice. I am grateful to Story Circle for the opportunity to submit my work for consideration.

CAROL TOOLE – DRIPPING SPRINGS TX

Carol Toole currently teaches reading and writing skills (remotely) to students grades 3-8. She has worked with children and parents for over 40 years, and is the author of a children's book, *Tara's Spring Wish*. Her love of language and children has inspired her current project, writing on speech development in young children, and how our enlivened speech helps keep us all in the present moment.

SUSAN J. TWEIT – SANTA FE NM

Susan J. Tweit is a plant biologist and the award-winning author of twelve books (including her memoir, *Walking Nature Home: A Life's Journey*, and *Colorado Scenic Byways*, winner of the Colorado Book Award), numerous magazine articles, and newspaper columns. Read her popular blog and learn about her books on her website. http://www.susanjtweit.com/meet-susan

JO VIRGIL – AUSTIN TX

Jo Virgil lives in Austin, and retired from a career in journalism and community relations. She has a Master of Journalism degree with a minor in Environmental Science, reflecting her love of writing and appreciation of nature, and has had stories and poetry published in various books, newspapers, and magazines, including Story Circle Network's publications. She lives by words she learned from one of her journalism professors: "Stories are what make us matter."

JUDE WALSH – DAYTON OH

Jude Walsh is an author, life coach, and writing teacher. As a coach, she works with women post divorce and with men and women wishing to reinvent themselves creatively and pivot to a new life. She teaches writing mindset and legacy writing. Jude is the author of the award-winning *Post-Divorce Bliss: Ending Us and Finding Me*. Her work is in numerous literary magazines and anthologies including *Chicken Soup For the Soul* and *The Magic of Memoir*. http://www.judewalshwrites.com http://secondbloomcoaching.com

LETTY WATT – NORMAN OK

Now that I'm retired (librarian and classroom teacher), staying healthy is a main priority in my life, so I will be able to enjoy the time I spend with family, friends. Without bells and deadlines I'm free to write and draw or just play. Even with the silent dis-ease in our world, I still find comfort in books, words, writing, and sharing. https://literallyletty.blogspot.com

CHRISTINA M. WELLS – ANNANDALE VA

Christina M. Wells is a writer, editor, and coach, who lives in Northern Virginia. She has published in Story Circle Journal, Northern Virginia Review, Crab Fat Magazine, bioStories, Big Muddy, Sinister Wisdom, and the blog of New Ventures West, among others. She is also included in the anthologies *Hashtag Queer Volume 3*, and *Is It Hot in Here, or is it Just Me?* She has an MA from University of Arkansas and a PhD from University of Maryland.

MARY JO WEST – SAN CLEMENTE CA

I am eighty-one years old and have been married for sixty-two years. I reside in San Clemente. I have three daughters and nine grandchildren. I started writing nine years ago and during that time, I have published my memoir, *No Reservations,* and a recipe book of my Italian-American family's favorites that have been handed down for generations. I am now writing fee verse poetry and short stories.

LINDA C. WISNIEWSKI – DOYLESTOWN PA

Linda C. Wisniewski is a former librarian, who lives with her retired scientist husband and their rescue cat, Denyse, in Doylestown. She has been a feature writer for two local newspapers, and teaches memoir workshops, and volunteers at the historic home of author Pearl S. Buck. Linda's memoir, *Off Kilter: A Woman's Journey to Peace with Scoliosis, Her Mother and Her Polish Heritage* was published in 2008. Her time travel novel, *Where the Stork Flies,* is forthcoming in 2020. https://www.lindawis.com

CHARLOTTE WLODKOWSKI – PITTSBURGH PA

Writing family stories was the beginning of recognizing a new form of communication for me — writing. Being a member of the Millvale Library Writing Group has developed my writing abilities and introduced me to various forms of writing. Currently, I am putting a book together that will include whimsical writings, inspirational essays, and fiction and nonfiction stories. It is my hope to open the minds and hearts of women.

JEANNE ZEEB-SCHECTER – VALLEY VILLAGE CA

I have been a homeopathic doctor for the past twenty-six years. During this pandemic, I retired. I belong to a local poetry class, a writing class, and I teach a Creative Life Writing class. I joined SCN four years ago. Currently, I am writing a nonfiction book on Homeopathy and Grief, as well as a historical novel about a healer. I am blessed to be married, have a daughter, four granddaughters, and seven great-grandchildren.

THELMA ZIRKELBACH – HOUSTON TX

Thelma Zirkelbach is a multi-published author of poetry, memoir, flash fiction and flash nonfiction, personal essay, and romantic suspense. She is also a recently retired speech-language pathologist. A native Texan, she lives in Houston and shares her home with Cassie, her intelligent and demanding cat.

ARIELA ZUCKER – ELLSWORTH ME

I was born in Jerusalem, Israel. My husband and I moved to the US on September 10, 2001; we were followed by three of our daughters. We live in Ellsworth in the motel we own and operate. I write mainly poetry and nonfiction, and have self-published three books, two about the motel experience and one about my family search. I currently facilitate an online writing group, as well as offer online writing classes. http://www.paperdragon.me

About the Editor

Susan F. Schoch, editor of *Real Women Write: Living on COVID Time*, is a freelance writer and editor specializing in personal history. She is author of *The Clay Connection*, a study of renowned ceramic artists Jim and Nan McKinnell, for the American Museum of Ceramic Art. She serves on the Board of Story Circle Network, reviews writing by and about women at Story Circle Book Reviews, and edited the 2017 SCN essay collection, *Inside and Out*. She has been editor of the annual *Real Women Write* anthology series since 2014. Susan lives in Colorado with her husband, Bob Smith, a ceramic artist and teacher. They have a large and loving family.

ABOUT STORY CIRCLE NETWORK: FOR WOMEN WITH STORIES TO TELL

Susan Wittig Albert

"We learn best to listen to our own voices if we are listening at the same time to other women, whose stories, for all our differences, turn out, if we listen well, to be our stories also."
— BARBARA DEMING

I'm going to use the personal pronoun when I tell you about SCN, because I am its founder and a current member of this wonderful organization. I am very proud of—and often amazed by—all we have done and continue to do.

Chartered in 1997 as a nonprofit organization, SCN is now twenty-three years old and still growing. Over the years, about 4,000 women in this country and elsewhere in the world have been members, and many times that number have participated in our programs. Our activities are funded by annual membership dues and fee-based programs, as well as the generous gifts and grants of friends and supporters. Our work is done by a very small paid staff and dozens of volunteers.

Story Circle Network is dedicated to helping women share the stories of their lives and to raising public awareness of the importance of women's personal histories. We carry out our mission through publications, websites, award programs, online and face-to-face classes and workshops, writing and reading circles, blogs, social media, and many woman-focused activities. We sponsor a biannual national women's writing conference, weekend writing retreats called "LifeLines," and a regular program of online classes and webinars. In 2020, our in-person activities have been postponed, but our online efforts have been greater than ever. We sponsor Story Circle Book Reviews, the largest and oldest women's book review site on the Internet, and also the annual Sarton Women's Writing Awards.

We encourage our members to publish their writing through our quarterly *Story Circle Journal*, annual *Real Women Write* anthology, and two blogs: "HerStories" and "One Woman's Day." In addition, SCN has published four collections of members' and others' writing: *With Courage and Common Sense: Memoirs from the Older Women's Legacy Circle; What Wildness is This: Women Write about the Southwest; Kitchen Table Stories*; and *Inside and Out.*

But what I have just told you about what we are doing at SCN today is likely to be out of date tomorrow, for we continue to explore new ways to serve the growing community of women writers and those who are interested in documenting and celebrating women's lives.

Visit us at https://www.storycircle.org/ where you can explore the many activities SCN has created to support women with stories to tell. We're here to help, because we believe in women's stories. Please join us.

BOOKS PUBLISHED BY STORY CIRCLE NETWORK

Inside and Out: Women's Truths, Women's Stories
edited by Susan F. Schoch

Real Women Write: Growing / Older
edited by Susan F. Schoch

Kitchen Table Stories
edited by Jane Ross

Starting Points
by Susan Wittig Albert

What Wildness is This: Women Write About the Southwest
edited by Susan Wittig Albert, Susan Hanson, Jan Epton Seale,
Paula Stallings Yost

With Courage and Common Sense:
Memoirs from the Older Women's Legacy Circle
edited by Susan Wittig Albert and Dayna Finet

Writing From Life
by Susan Wittig Albert

True Words from Real Women, the SCN Anthology, 2009-2014
edited by Amber Lea Starfire, Mary Jo Doig, Susan F. Schoch

Real Women Write: Sharing Our Stories, Sharing Our Lives,
the SCN Anthology, 2015-2018
edited by Susan F. Schoch

"This is precisely the time when artists go to work.

There is no time for despair, no place for self-pity,

no need for silence, no room for fear.

We speak, we write, we do language.

That is how civilizations heal."

— Toni Morrison

...by, for, and about women.

This book was designed using Adobe Garamond, Copperplate,
and Eccentric fonts.
Designed and typeset by Sherry Wachter:
sherry@sherrywachter.com